✻ American Quilts ✻

BOOK 3: DANIEL'S STORY

First Aladdin Paperbacks edition March 2001

Text copyright © 2001 by Susan E. Kirby

Aladdin Paperbacks
An imprint of Simon & Schuster
Children's Publishing Division
1230 Avenue of the Americas
New York, NY 10020

Printed and bound in the United States of America

2 4 6 8 10 9 7 5 3 1

Library of Congress Cataloging–in–Publication Data

Kirby, Susan E.
Daniel's story / by Susan E. Kirby.
p.   cm. — (American quilts ; #3)
Summary: Great-grandmother Tandy tells Lacey about a quilt given to their ancestor, Daniel, who, upset by the changes after his grandfather's death, leaves Illinois for South Dakota in 1891 to find his father, and he learns about the Sioux Ghost Dance firsthand.
ISBN: 0-689-80971-9
1. Ghost dance—Juvenile fiction. 2. Dakota Indians—Juvenile fiction. [1. Ghost dance—Fiction. 2. Dakota Indians—Fiction. 3. Frontier and pioneer life—Fiction. 4. Indians of North America—Great Plains—Fiction. 5. Quilts—Fiction.] I. Title.
PZ7.K63353 Dan 2000 [Fic]—dc21   00-058294

To Tracy, with love,
To Reggie,
And to happily ever afters

Acknowledgments

Sylvester Keller, Train Restoration, Monticello, Illinois
Thank you for the stroll through the graveyard of trains
waiting to be restored, and for sharing your knowledge of an
earlier era of train travel, baggage cars, and 'riding the rods.'

J. Clifford Wilcox
The time and pictures you shared of the Tile Factory
School at Funks Grove, as well as the photos of the Tile
Factory and Lumber Mill were a great aid as I developed
the setting for *Daniel's Story*.

Bill Case, curator, Funk Prairie Home, Shirley, Illinois
The log cabin quilt at Prairie Home fits as if custom-made
for *Daniel's Story* and makes a beautiful frame on the
cover. I appreciate your enthusiasm for Prairie Home,
history children can visit and borrow from in their own
creative writing.

I am also indebted to the late Lena Zoeller for sharing
her knowledge of the Tile Factory School. Lena knew the
school from both sides of the desk. Having attended there
as a child, she returned years later as a teacher and
remained until 1947, when Funks Grove Tile Factory
School went the way of so many rural one-room schools.
Lena's memories were vivid. As she shared stories of
schoolmates and school yard pranks and her esteem for a
much beloved teacher, I could smell mittens drying on
the stove and hear mischievous children chant *Nate,
Nate, bald on the pate*.

Dear Reader:

Daniel and the Tandy clan are fictional. But I did borrow from family history in the death of Daniel's grandfather. My great-grandfather Isaac Funk II was struck and killed by a train at the Funks Grove crossing in a similar manner. Another story element plucked from family history is the syrup camp. Maple syrup has been made at Funks Grove, Illinois, since the pioneering days of my great-great-grandfather. But it wasn't until 1891 that a commercial syrup camp was established by the Funk family. The business, operated now by my brother and his wife, is something of a landmark along historic Route 66. A few miles north in rural Shirley at the Funk Prairie Home, which is open to the public, you can view the Log Cabin quilt that was my inspiration for Gram Harmony's Log Cabin quilt.

But like Daniel, you will have to travel a bit to reach the heart of the story. It lies in South Dakota, for it was there while visiting the Crazy Horse monument and visitors' center that I first learned of the Sioux Star quilt and Native American quilting traditions. Sioux and other Plains Indians adapted their skill in needlework to quilt-making when buffalo robes and other animal skin covers grew scarce. Initially, traders provided cloth, and mission schools and mission societies taught the craft. The artistry Native women had practiced in traditional bedcoverings and clothing adapted beautifully to quilts. Variations of the Sioux Star pattern continue to be highly favored. They are rich in Native symbols, and a medium for passing down from generation to generation Sioux artistry, history, and culture.

Whether used in burial rites, decorating, gifting, honoring, fund-raising, or simply to warm a cold night, there is attached to the Sioux Star quilt a sense of "belongingness" that warms the soul. Against the escalating tensions that culminate in the tragedy at Wounded Knee, it is this "belongingness" that sinks a hook in Daniel's heart. I chose not to sanitize the language of that day. The words from history's headlines expose the fear, mistrust, arrogance, and ignorance that advanced the tragedy. To gloss over the ugliness of it would be an injustice to the memory of those who died and a distortion of the prejudices that existed on both sides.

A carpenter from Galilee was once asked, "Who is my neighbor?" The question prompted a story known as the parable of the Good Samaritan. No one asked, "Who is my enemy?" We assume we know the enemy. But do we?

I urge you, dear reader, to visit Wounded Knee, South Dakota. If you can't do so in person, journey there through recorded history. Let the past speak to you. I hope it moves you to write a story of your own that conveys a message of "belongingness."

May it fall on listening ears.

Until next time, my friend,

Susan E. Kirby

✷ **American Quilts** ✷

BOOK 3: DANIEL'S STORY

✷ ✷ ✷ SUSAN E. KIRBY ✷ ✷ ✷

ALADDIN PAPERBACKS

NEW YORK   LONDON   TORONTO   SYDNEY   SINGAPORE

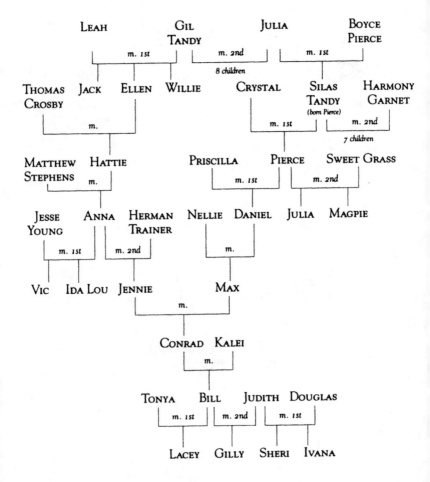

Prologue

Eleven-year-old Lacey Tandy spread sunbonnet girls and overall boys over her bed. One of these days she would join the white squares to which they were stitched to make a quilt top.

"Each one is from my family tree," Lacey said as her stepsister Sheri looked on. "This is Julia Pierce Tandy. She was a pioneer. I chose blue because that was her favorite color. This is her son, Silas, in yellow overalls. And this is Ellen Tandy. She liked blue, too. The one in the yellow dress is Ellen's daughter, Hattie. Gram told me all about her. She was very brave. I wish I could touch the cloth and she'd come to life and I could meet her in person."

Sheri rolled her eyes. "You're plain silly about your old dead Tandys."

Lacey flushed. Sheri was better with a basketball than with her imagination.

"So what color are you using for me?" asked Sheri.

The question caught Lacey by surprise. Sheri had been her stepsister for over a year now. Ivana, too. But they weren't blood relatives. Did they belong on her family quilt?

"Make me orange," said Sheri. She tucked her basketball under her arm. "I'm going out to shoot some hoops.

Are you coming? Or or you going to sit here and drool over your Tandys?"

"Neither," said Lacey. "I'm going out to the farm to see Gram."

The farm where Lacey's great-grandmother lived had been in the Tandy family for seven generations. The big trees in the yard showed their autumn colors. But to Lacey's eyes, Gram Jennie looked like spring, always bright and cheerful. She was gray-haired, bespectacled, and spry. A gifted storyteller and the keeper of the family quilts, she passed out hugs like cookies and smelled of roses and face powder.

"Dad said he'd pick me up about dark," Lacey said when Gram Jennie had hugged a giggle out of her.

"A whole day together. Wonderful!" The porch swing bumped as Gram got to her feet. "How is everyone?"

"Fine." Lacey followed her into the comfortable old farmhouse. "Ivana stayed all night with a friend. Dad and Sheri are going to rake leaves, and Judith has a doctor's appointment."

"How are her feet?"

"Swollen," said Lacey. "She gained two pounds in a week. She's going to work another week, then quit until the baby comes."

"It won't be long now," said Gram.

Six weeks, according to Judith. Lacey was trying very hard to get used to the idea of a new baby. Gram said if you made up your mind to love it, the feeling would follow. "I wish I knew whether it's going to be a boy or girl. Then I could make it a block for my quilt."

"That's all right, Lacey. We have plenty of past Tandys to keep you busy until the baby comes," said Gram.

"That reminds me, Gram." Lacey perched on the old humpback trunk in Gram's parlor. She unzipped her book bag and took out her sunbonnet girls. "Does orange clash?" she asked.

"With what, dear?" Gram asked, looking on.

"My Tandy quilt. It's Sheri's favorite color. But I think it sort of . . . well . . . I'm not sure it belongs," finished Lacey.

Gram peered over the tops of her glasses. "Sheri? Or the color orange?"

Heat rose to Lacey's face. She hugged her knees. "We don't fight so much now. It's just that . . . she isn't really a Tandy. Not by blood."

Gram patted her cheek. "Hop up, honey. I have something to show you."

Lacey loved looking through the old quilts. Some were very fragile and had to be handled with care. She shifted to her feet and helped Gram open the trunk. The first quilt Gram withdrew was a block quilt, made of ribbons and satins pieced together in narrow strips.

"Log Cabin," Lacey said, recognizing the pattern.

"That's right," said Gram. She pulled out a second quilt. It was a single eight-point star on a background of white. Lacey frowned, trying to think what it might be called.

"It's a Sioux Star quilt," Gram told her. "But in our family we've always called it Belongingness."

"Belongingness?" echoed Lacey.

Gram closed the trunk. She draped both quilts over the lid and patted them fondly. "You'll remember that your great-great-great-great-grandfather Silas Tandy was not a Tandy by blood. He was a Pierce. He took the name when his mother married Gil Tandy. Silas named his first-born son Pierce Tandy. Pierce Tandy had a boy named Daniel. Daniel was your Grampa Max's father. He gave me Belongingness. Would you like to hear about it?"

Lacey nodded and settled on the floor with her sunbonnet girls while Gram sat down at her quilting frame.

Chapter One

January 1890

Daniel Tandy was dark-eyed, scant, and scrawny. He was a comma in a compound sentence of land-rich Tandys. His father was a question mark off taming the Wild West. His mother was underground. And his grandparents were periods.

"Grampa?" Daniel said one morning as he pored over his sketchbook. "I was thinking I'd go visit Dad when it gets to be summer."

"South Dakota?" Grampa Silas unfolded himself from his chair by the stove. "I'm too old, and you're too young to cross the country alone."

Period. Fixed and firm as a mended fence. If he wouldn't reach into his deep pockets, asking Gram Harmony was a waste of breath.

Commas bend. Sometimes they yield. But they have heels, by hook. Without a word, Daniel dug his in. He *would* go to South Dakota if he had to sketch his way there.

Robinlike, Daniel kept his ear to the ground. Late in January, the worm wiggled. The worm came by way of Jack, who was Daniel's best friend and the grandson of Grampa Silas's stepbrother, Jack Tandy.

"Earl's going to make syrup next month. You want to help?" Jack asked.

That easily, the means of earning a ticket west were within Daniel's grasp.

Days later, Daniel tramped through the woods with Jack. Thawing earth and dead leaves bled through the thin, wet snow underfoot. He dropped to one knee, pressed the drill bit into bark, and rotated the brace. Maple shavings scattered on the breeze.

Jack charged the hole with a wooden sap spile and hammer. Daniel rubbed a watery eye and walked on. He didn't know maples by bark, but Jack's brother Earl had left buckets beneath the trees to be tapped.

"Hey! You're getting ahead of yourself," hollered Jack.

Daniel glanced back and saw he had missed a bucket. He was chilled, his knees wet and muddy clear through his long-handles. "You drill it," he said, and offered Jack the brace and bit.

"You," said Jack. "You're closer to the ground."

Jack was a year older than Daniel, a head taller, and stoutly built.

He squatted like a frog about to jump while Daniel drilled the hole. Jack cleaned out the shavings with a twig and took another spile from the lard pail.

The spiles were as big around as a man's finger. They were long, lightweight, and channeled to carry maple sap from the tree to the bucket on the ground. Grampa Silas had helped Earl whittle them from elderberry and sumac. Earl was fresh out of school. Tandylike, he was set on making a living off the land, even if the land was in trees.

"How much is Earl paying us?" asked Daniel.

"Not much. He's cheap." Jack urged the spile into the hole with the hammer, then set the bucket beneath it.

A train rattled by on the nearby Chicago & Alton Railroad tracks and slowed for the Funks Grove crossing.

"Must be the nooner," said Jack. "My belly's growling."

Daniel wiped his dripping nose. "Want to walk to the store and warm up?"

"I don't have any money."

"We can put some cheese on Grampa's account. He won't care," said Daniel.

Walker's Store was a rough-sawed wood and tin-roofed affair with a wide front window and living quarters in back for young Mr. Walker and his wife. It stood in a clearing near the rural crossing where the tracks ran through sprawling timber.

A handful of men climbed off the train. They pulled coats on over their red bandannas, cinder-pocked shirts, and coveralls. Leaving the tinder taking on water, they ambled toward Walker's. Daniel crossed in front of the idling engine. It hissed and popped and sent a thin ribbon of steam floating into the trees.

Jack dropped his red head back, squinting at the engine. "You ever been up there?"

"No," said Daniel. "Have you?"

"Nope. How about it?"

"You mean, *now*?"

"Sure, now," said Jack.

"What if they catch us?"

"They won't."

Daniel frowned up at the engine. He shifted from one cold foot to the other.

Jack twisted his mouth to one side and sniffed. "What's that again about your trader, trapper, tracklaying, Indian-scouting, gold-prospecting daddy?"

"I never said he laid track. I said he hunted buffalo to feed the men who built the railroad across—"

"The plains. I know." Jack bumped Daniel with his shoulder. "So did Fierce Pierce get all the guts in the family?"

Walker's door slammed shut behind the train crew. Daniel eyed the monster engine and gave in with a shrug.

Jack's windburned freckles bunched into a grin. He set aside his hammer and pail of spiles and reached for the bottom rung of the steps that scaled the engine. Daniel dropped his tools and scrambled up after him. It was warm inside the engine cab.

"What're you buying with your syrup money?" Daniel asked, thawing his hands at the firebox door.

"Bicycle, maybe." Jack gripped a brass knob. He thunked a gauge. "How about you?"

"I'm going to buy a train ticket to South Dakota."

"To see your dad?"

Daniel nodded.

"Uncle Silas know?"

"No. Don't tell anybody, okay?"

"'Course not. Tandys never tell on Tandys," said Jack.

It was true. Of Jack, anyway. For all his cajoling and

ca-jamming and half-cocked Tandy temper, he was a clam when it came to secrets.

Jack spit on the sooty window and rubbed a patch clean with his coat sleeve. "Look there, a bird's-eye view. Almost see clear to Indian country."

The farm where Daniel lived with his grandparents was a half mile due east. He couldn't see it for the woodlands in between.

Jack nudged him. "Look who's coming. Chaldea."

A woman with flaming hair and flapping black skirts pedaled across Timber Creek bridge on a bicycle. Her name wasn't really Chaldea. Miss Maralee Jennings, that was her name. She lived in the woods and gathered bark and roots and such. What she couldn't find in the wild, she grew and dried for teas and poultices and potions. "Remedies," she called them.

"Earl says she reads the future in the stars," said Jack. "He says when she talks to the dead, they talk back."

"How?"

"Spirit to spirit."

Daniel prodded with the tip of his tongue the space between his front teeth, watching Chaldea's bicycle wobble over thawing ruts. She stopped at the crossing, looked at the train and then south to open track, and pedaled ahead.

The steam whistle shrieked. Daniel jumped.

Chaldea, too. She veered hard to the right. The front wheel of her bicycle jammed between rail and rocks. She went down in a flash of black cape, dingy petticoats, and scattered remedies, and lurched off the rails on her knees.

Jack let go of the whistle chain and held his sides, laughing.

Chaldea bounded to her shoddy feet, gaped up at the engine, and thrust a bony arm in the air. Two fingers arched out of a woolen mitten, wiggly as snakes poised to strike.

Daniel ducked to the floor.

Jack jerked him up again. "Crew's coming!"

To the west, men poured from the store. Daniel flung himself out after Jack. He missed a step on his way down. Jack broke his fall. They scrambled to their feet, grabbed their tree-tapping tools, and dashed into the timber just ahead of the train crew's garbled shouts.

Chapter Two

"Yikes! She hexed you!" yelped Jack.

Daniel looked back to see Chaldea pointing after him with those same two fingers. For the first time ever, he outran Jack. He crashed through the trees and over fallen logs and didn't slow until the timber gave way to Grampa's farm.

The outbuildings and handsome two-story house with its deep verandas and topknot catwalk gleamed white on the melting prairie. Daniel dropped the brace and bit on the closed-in summer porch and bolted into the sunny kitchen. Jack tumbled in after him. They fell together in a panting heap.

Grampa's niece Hattie was at the stove. Hattie's mother, Ellen, who had died the year before in Kansas, was a stepsister to Grampa Silas. Short and dark-haired, Hattie tapped her wooden spoon against a steamy kettle and darted them a keen-eyed glance. "What's the problem?" she asked.

"Chaldea!" wheezed Jack.

"That's Miss Jennings to you," corrected Hattie. Her green eyes narrowed. "What about her?"

"She fell off . . . her bicycle . . . going over . . . the railroad tracks," panted Daniel.

"Did you help her up?"

"With remedies blowing every witchity way?" said Jack. "That's a good way to stumble into a spell."

"Spells-bells, Jackfrey! I've got no time for your nonsense," exclaimed Hattie. "Are you staying for lunch? Then get out of those muddy overshoes."

Hattie crossed to the foot of the back stairs. "Aunt Harmony? Lunch is ready," she shouted into the mouth of a talking tube.

The tube, hidden by the plushly papered wall, traveled up the staircase, into the sewing room and the bedrooms beyond. It took such a shout to be heard through it, a good ear could catch messages out of the air without the tube.

"Not so fast," Hattie said as Daniel unbuttoned his coat. "Run outside first and see what's keeping your grandfather."

With four daughters of her own, mothering came naturally to Hattie. As did giving orders. Daniel was good at taking them. So were Hattie's daughters, which accounted for Hattie being able to keep her own house and Gram Harmony's, too.

Daniel fastened his coat and trudged out again. There was no one in the cattle barn but his black cat, Shadow. Daniel stooped to tickle Shadow's ears, then tramped on to the stables. "Grampa?"

His voice echoed down the dim, straw-strewn corridor between stalls. He heard one horse stamping straw, and another rubbing against the stall, but no human sounds.

Daniel made a quick search of the log cabin toolshed and other outbuildings, then cut through the yard again and on to the springhouse. Just short of the door, a figure lay crumpled in the snow.

A cold spasm gripped Daniel's belly. It hit the air in a shout that brought Hattie and Jack to the back door. Daniel hunkered beside his grandfather, his heart pipping like an engine blowing off steam.

Hattie raced across the yard with Jack at her heels. "What happened? Uncle Silas? Can you hear me?"

Grampa Silas's eyes fluttered open as Hattie fell beside him. His mouth moved. But the wind tore away his words. A tremor shook him as he tried to sit up.

"He's chilled to the bone. Give me your coat, Daniel," urged Hattie.

Daniel helped cover his grandfather with his coat. But it slid off again as Grampa Silas turned on his side and vomited in the snow.

Jack gagged and backed away.

Daniel's stomach rolled, too. Hattie nudged him out of the way. She steadied his grandfather with wrap-around arms and patted him, murmuring until the retching stopped.

"Stomach convulsions," Grampa Silas said in a shuddering voice. "Knocked my legs out from under me."

Hattie gave him her handkerchief. "You didn't injure yourself falling?" she asked as he wiped his mouth.

"Help me up." Grampa brushed her questions aside and stretched a hand to Daniel.

"Jack's stronger. Help me, Jack," said Hattie, on her

haunches, poised to lift. "Get on the other side of him. That's the way. Gently!"

Grampa moaned and held his middle and staggered upward. Wrinkled and weathered, he was a stickler for good posture. But he couldn't straighten today. He moved on faltering steps for the back door, head down, arms cradling his middle.

Daniel reached for his coat and saw his grandfather's gold watch glittering in the melting snow. The glass fell in pieces as he picked it up. He held it to his ear. It had stopped ticking.

"Send one of the men for Doc Ritter, Daniel," Hattie called to him from the back steps. "Hurry!"

Chapter Three

South of the barns and outbuildings was a boarding-house. From springtime until the crops were gathered in, it was full of men who worked planting, tending, and harvesting. Many were young and single and returned to their families after the crops were in. But a few stayed to help on the home place and care for the livestock over the winter.

Daniel found a dozen men sitting down to lunch in the boardinghouse kitchen. One hurried to the horse barn with Daniel and saddled up. Daniel watched him ride off to fetch the doctor, then returned to the house.

Jack was at the kitchen table. He looked up from scooping chicken and noodles with a fork and a thick slice of bread. "Cousin Hattie said eat. She's upstairs helping Aunt Harmony get Uncle Silas into bed."

"How is he?"

"Still complaining about his stomach," said Jack.

Daniel's stomach hurt, too. He wasn't sure food would fix it. But he filled a plate, joined Jack, and slid the broken watch across the table. "I found it where Grampa fell."

Jack turned the watch over in his hand. His blue gaze darted from the watch face back to Daniel. "Look where the hands stopped. Seven minutes after twelve."

"So?"

"About the time Chaldea jumped up and hexed you, I'd say."

"*Me?*" blurted Daniel, alarmed. "What about *you?*"

"Could be she overshot her mark and missed us both," said Jack. He dropped his head back and pointed to the ceiling. "Listen."

The heat rose through an iron grate and warmed the sewing room on the second floor. Gram and Grampa's bedchamber adjoined the sewing room. The door between the rooms must have been open, for Daniel could hear Grampa retching again.

"That doesn't mean anything. He's had bellyaches before," reasoned Daniel.

"Bad as this?"

It did sound bad. Daniel rubbed the chill off his neck. He doused himself with false courage and argued, "He'll be better. Once the doctor comes and gives him medicine."

"I hope so, because if he doesn't . . ." Jack broke off whatever he had been about to say. He slid the watch across the table, then got up and filled his plate again.

When Dr. Ritter arrived, Jack pulled on his boots and coat and trekked off with his tapping tools to find Earl. Daniel filled the coal bucket and dumped the ash pan as he waited for Gram to come downstairs and tell him what was wrong with Grampa.

He was still waiting when Hattie ushered Dr. Ritter into the kitchen. She filled a plate for the doctor and questioned him about Grampa while he ate.

Daniel's Story

Dr. Ritter used big words. Mostly unfamiliar ones. Daniel waited for a break in the conversation. But before he could question Hattie, she sent him upstairs with a tray for Gram.

The damask draperies were drawn in the bedroom. A fire burned behind the ornate screen on the hearth. Gram Harmony sat in a velvet-upholstered chair between the bed and the fireplace. Her hair was piled on her head as smooth and pale and gleamy as butter fresh from Hattie's medallion-shaped butter mold.

Gram was a good bit younger than Grampa, with scars instead of wrinkles. In the glow of the fire, they trailed over her face like melting wax. She had come by her scars and her lame leg as a young woman a few years before the War Between the States. At the time, Mount Hope, where she taught school, was a stop on the Underground Railroad for escaping slaves. Hattie, just a girl then, had been part of the woodland accident. Wearing shoes she had traded with an escaping slave girl, she had laid a false trail that bloodhounds and slave hunters followed. The dead tree Hattie had climbed to safety fell on Gram, who was carrying a lantern, and on Chaldea's little brother. Daniel didn't remember the boy's name, only that he had died, crushed by the tree that had maimed Gram Harmony.

Unlike Hattie, Gram never talked about it except to date long-ago events in terms of before and after the accident. She was a schoolteacher and single *before*. Marriage to Silas Tandy came *after*. With it, she became a stepmom to Daniel's motherless father, which made her Daniel's stepgram.

But "step" was just a detail. Like "scar." It was only Grampa lying there so still and pale with quilts to his knobby chin that made Daniel think of it. "Gram?" He held up the tray.

Gram Harmony touched her finger to her lips and reached for her cane. She motioned for Daniel to follow her into the adjoining room, the room over the kitchen.

The sewing room was small compared to the others in the house. It had once been a nursery. Daniel didn't remember sleeping there. But he had. In infancy, he had lost his mother to consumption and his grieving father to the west. These days, the crib held Gram's quilting projects and linens and fabric scraps and mending and sewing widgets.

Gram's treadle machine was folded into its black-lacquered cabinet beneath the window, where the light was strong. Daniel set the tray down on top of it and moved a chair for Gram.

"Thank you, dear," she said, keeping her voice low. "What about you? Have you eaten?"

"With Jack," Daniel said so she wouldn't fuss. "He had to go back to work for Earl."

"I thought you were helping, too," said Gram.

"I did, all morning. What's wrong with Grampa?"

"Dr. Ritter says it's liver complaint, complicated by impoverished blood."

Daniel had heard that much from Hattie and the doctor. "What's that mean?" he asked.

"Poor," said Gram. She spread the linen napkin over her lap.

The twitch in her hands was more revealing than her words. Daniel's fears were fertile soil. Questions sprang up like weeds. Poisonous ones. He couldn't uproot them. Neither could he bring himself to ask.

Gram barely touched her food. Daniel returned with her to the bedroom. Grampa shivered under the covers. His face was colorless, his breathing labored. Air went in a wheeze, and out a putter.

Daniel crossed the landing and tidied his bedroom without being told. Or tried, anyway. There was more stuff than there were places to put it. For years now, his father had been sending him things from the west. An Indian headdress. A buckskin shirt, fringed and beaded. Leggings and moccasins, too. Assorted Indian tools and utensils. He also had a gold nugget his father had found while prospecting in the Black Hills. It wasn't big. But it was real. He kept it and other treasures in the saddlebag his father had used years ago when he carried the mail for the Pony Express.

Daniel retrieved his sketchbook from the saddlebag. He turned back the quilts, stretched out on the cold sheet, and gripped the pencil. Lead flowed over the page, pouring out the image of Grampa in the snow. But it was too lifelike.

Daniel turned the page. He drew Chaldea falling off her bicycle. Then he wrote his father a letter:

Dad,

It's me, Daniel. I'm fine. But Grampa's not. He got sick today and fell down outside. I found him. We got him inside, and the doctor came. He has attacking bile, and liver's complaining. Oh, and something's wrong with his blood. Gram says he's doing poorly.
Maybe if you were to come home, he would feel better.

Your son, Daniel

Gram gave Daniel an envelope and a stamp. He tucked the letter and picture inside. His father didn't write often. But when he did, he always remarked upon the drawings Daniel sent.

Daniel took the sealed letter downstairs, where Hattie was pummeling and shredding a piece of raw beef. She measured the meat shavings into a mason jar, covered the jar, and put it in a saucepan of water on the stove.

"Where are you going?" Hattie asked as he reached for his coat.

"The store," Daniel said, shrugging into it. Outgoing mail was gathered at Walker's Store and sent along by train. "I wrote Dad and told him about Grampa being sick."

Hattie patted his shoulder. "Wear your overshoes. As long as you're going, I need caraway, lemons, and alum."

"Write it down," said Daniel.

Hattie tore off a bit of brown paper. There was a knock at the back door. "That's probably Matthew," she said, scribbling out her list. "Let him in, would you, Daniel?"

Matthew was Hattie's husband. Sometimes, when it was cold, he picked her up so she wouldn't have to walk home.

Daniel crossed the kitchen and the unheated summer porch in a single overshoe. But he dropped the other just short of the threshold. For it wasn't Matthew standing on the other side of the screen door. It was Chaldea.

Her gaze leaped over him like blue flames in smoked chimney glass.

Chapter Four

Daniel stumbled over his overshoe and fell flat on his back.

Chaldea charged through the door. Her crackly shoes stopped an inch from his face. "You!" she hissed, with an accusing thrust of her bony hand.

Daniel recoiled from her wagging fingers. "It wasn't me, it was Jack!" he shrieked, and flung his arms over his eyes.

"Demons!" Chaldea lifted her skirts and stepped over him.

Daniel's skin tingled hot, needling at the brush of her dragging hem. He smelled sage. Wrinkled his nose. Held his breath.

Chaldea swept into the warmth of Hattie's surprised greeting, leaving the door ajar. Daniel rolled away and to his knees, listening.

"You couldn't have come at a better time. Or should I say worse? It's Uncle Silas's liver complaint," Hattie said in a blithery gust. "He hasn't kept a drop down all day."

"Caraway is good for irritable stomach and bowel." Chaldea's voice rustled like dry herbs. "Is that him coughing?"

"Yes. He's caught a chill."

"A pinch of alum in a glass of water will help. That and Imperial drink. Both are good for throat irritation."

"I know. I have cream of tartar, but I don't have any lemons. There's a problem with his blood, too," said Hattie.

"Impoverished?"

"Yes. I'm making beef tea."

"Don't begin the tea just yet. A mustard plaster will help his stomach discomfort. I know just the thing for poor blood."

"You're a godsend, Maralee," exclaimed Hattie. "Daniel? Now, where did he get off to? Daniel?"

Daniel picked himself up off the summer porch floor, certain it was not God who had sent her.

Hattie swung the door wide. "There you are! All I need from the store is fresh lemons. Miss Jennings has everything else."

Beyond her, Chaldea was sorting herbs, roots, and potions on the table. Her hair spilled over her shoulders in shreds, the same bloodred as the meat simmering in the jar on the stove.

Daniel gaped at the remedies. As if from a distance, he heard Hattie hurrying him. "And close the door. You're letting in cold air," she finished.

Daniel was glad to go and, at the same time, reluctant to be gone. He saddled his horse, Boots, and arrived at the store in short order.

"If it isn't young Master Tandy," Mr. Walker said, leaning on his broom. "What's this I hear about you and your freckle-faced cousin causing Miss Jennings's bicycle to bolt?"

It was Chaldea who had told Mr. Walker. Daniel arrived home to find her bicycle gone. Matthew's team was coming up the lane.

Daniel ducked into the barn and dawdled, putting Boots away.

Hattie came looking and cornered him there. "So you climbed up where you had no business," she scolded, her arms fluttering beneath her cape like flapping wings. "That was a mean stunt, frightening poor Maralee."

"How was it she knew what Grampa would need?" Daniel asked, lifting his head.

"What do you mean, 'knew'?"

"If it's a spell, and it's making Grampa sick, he shouldn't take her medicine, should he?"

"A spell? Whatever gave you such an idea?"

"Jack says Chaldea hexed me."

"Jackfrey!" Hattie spit Jack's family nickname. "I should have guessed. I could tan his hide when he does this to you—and yours, too—for letting him."

"But he said—"

"Surely you know you can't believe everything Jack tells you!"

"Yes, but—"

"Then why, when his imagination runs toward yarns and mischief, don't you sift what he's saying and decide for yourself instead of being so gullible?"

"Sometimes he's right. What if she *did* hex me?"

"She *didn't*, Daniel. She's a sad, lonely woman doing

her best to get by. You boys and your mischief—"

"But if she did . . . you know . . . and if it caught Grampa by accident—"

"Would you listen to me?" Hattie gripped Daniel's arm and pulled him around where the lantern light was stronger. "She did not hex you, or Uncle Silas, either. If she's odd and cold and hard-shelled, all I can say is she didn't set out to be. Lord knows she's had more than her share of heartache. It's shaped her, and not for the better. But that doesn't excuse you and Jack for abusing her."

"Hattie?" Daniel whispered as her stinging words settled in the frosty air.

"What is it, Daniel?"

"You still didn't answer."

"Answer what?" she said with a generous portion of Tandy impatience.

"How did she know what remedies to bring?"

"Maralee always knows," said Hattie. "When it comes to nature's medicine, she is the best around. So no more talk about hexes. You hear?"

Daniel sighed.

"Good," Hattie said, though he hadn't spoken. "Aunt Harmony won't want to leave Uncle Silas's bedside. But we'll pick you up for church tomorrow, and you be sure to apologize to Maralee while you're there. Is that clear?"

"Yes, ma'am."

"Let it be a lesson to you to do your own thinking. It's lazy, letting Jack do it for you," she added.

"Yes, ma'am," he said again.

"That's my boy." Hattie's restraining hand gentled. "Matthew's waiting on me. You go on inside and eat. I put supper on a tray for you and Aunt Harmony. I'll see you in the morning," she said, and patted him, cotton-comfort forgiveness in her touch.

Daniel shuffled out of the barn after her. Matthew waved to him from the springboard wagon. He was a husky fellow with a crop of rusty hair, a dapper mustache, and a case of the wanderlust. That's what Gram said about him, anyway. After Hattie settled onto the seat beside Matthew, he smooched to the team. They moved ahead, hooves plucking at the frosty ground.

Inside, Daniel shed his wraps, found the tray of leftovers, and carried it upstairs. Grampa was propped up in bed, sipping what looked like water. He was so weak, Gram had to help him hold the glass. When he had huddled under the covers again, she touched her wrist to his brow and said encouraging things. "Maralee and her remedies," she murmured. "She'll set you right."

"Could you put out that lamp? It's hurting my eyes," Grampa said, shielding his eyes.

He didn't mention the train incident. Neither did Gram. Daniel supposed that meant Hattie hadn't told him. Maybe she wouldn't, as long as he apologized to Chaldea.

Chapter Five

Daniel went to church with Hattie's family on Sunday. But Chaldea wasn't there. The preacher had heard about Grampa Silas being sick. He asked folks to keep him in their prayers, and when Daniel got up on Monday morning, Grampa was feeling a little better.

Hattie came alone on foot.

"Where's Matthew?" Daniel asked as she traded her coat for an apron.

"Home with Anna," said Hattie.

"Why? Is she sick?"

"She has a chest cold. It looks like it could snow, and I don't want her out in the weather."

Anna was Hattie and Matthew's youngest girl. She was six, and went to the same school as Daniel. Occasionally, when it was very cold, Daniel caught a ride with Matthew and Anna. The rest of the time, he rode Boots to school.

On Monday, Hattie fixed breakfast. Daniel ate, then bundled up, saddled Boots, and rode south across frozen fields. The tall steam stack of the Funks Grove Tile and Brick Factory and Sawmill loomed in the distance.

Weather-making clouds gathered overhead, chilling

the air. Daniel urged Boots into a trot. He dismounted two miles later near the barrow pit. It was a hole in the ground from which clay was dug for making bricks and tile.

There was a two-story brick house next to the school. Beyond that sprawled lumber sheds, the steam stack, and buildings that housed steam-powered equipment. Brown grass made whiskers in the snowcapped earth kilns where bricks and tiles were dried. The lumber company and manufacturing plant covered a dozen acres. It was bordered on the west by the Chicago & Alton Railroad tracks. In fair weather, the grounds hummed with horsepower, men, and machinery. But today, all was quiet.

Daniel turned Boots into the pony shed. He shivered his way over the stiles and through the school yard and stamped muddy snow off his feet at the door. There were two halls off the front entry. Daniel flung his coat and scarf over a hook in the boys' hall and left his lunch pail on the shelf with his hat.

The Tile Factory School was an ungraded school. That meant all grades were taught by one teacher, Mr. Nate Nelson. His desk sat on a platform up front. Behind the desk, a blackboard stretched across the back wall. Maps and charts were tacked over parts of the board.

A big, coal-burning stove dominated the room. There was a row of small, short windows high on one wall, and big, generous windows with a view of the school yard on the opposite wall. All of the windows were frosty. Mr. Nelson had scraped one clean and was watching the children arrive. He was a round, bald-headed man with a kindly face and an even manner. The wooden floor creaked as he turned and greeted Daniel. "It looks as if I could get snow for my birthday," he said.

"Today's your birthday?" asked Daniel.

Mr. Nelson nodded and crossed to the stove. He picked up the coal bucket and went into the back room, where the coal was stored.

Daniel's desk was in the middle row. He lifted the wooden lid, retrieved a notebook and a pencil, and drew Mr. Nelson a birthday picture. It showed him with a book in one hand and a coal bucket in the other. He lost himself in his drawing. When he looked up again, the room was crowded with children, many of them Tandy cousins. Some were Gram and Grampa Silas's grandchildren. Others were the grandchildren of Grampa's half brothers and sisters. And still others, like Jack, were the grandchildren of Grampa Silas's stepbrothers, Jack and Willie.

Across the top of his card Daniel scribbled, HAPPY BIRTHDAY, MR. NELSON.

Jack raced in just as Mr. Nelson rang the bell. There was no time to talk, and when recess came, Mr. Nelson said it was too cold for outdoors play. He hung a map of the United States over the blackboard and taught them a geography game.

"Buckeye," Mr. Nelson gave a clue. Then, with his hickory stick, he pointed to a state.

"Ohio!" Jack called it out first.

"That's right. Now you take a turn, Jack," said Mr.

Nelson. "First, a clue about the state. Then indicate its place on the map."

Jack took the stick. "Brand-new state. There's gold in the hills," he said, moving the pointer west.

"South Dakota!" shouted Daniel.

It was the place Daniel's father now called home, the state Jack knew Daniel would know. Daniel shot forward, took the pointer from Jack, and tried to think of a state Jack was sure to know. He studied the map a moment. "Where Hattie married Matthew," he said.

"Kansas!" Jack hollered just as the pointer hit the map.

Several other Tandy cousins hollered it, too, though none as fast as Jack. They were quick to object.

"The clues must be about the states, not your relatives, Daniel," agreed Mr. Nelson. He sat down at his desk.

"Let's say anyone who gives a bad clue has to put his nose to the blackboard," said one of the girls.

"Daniel!" the children chorused.

On his way to the board, Daniel dropped his birthday greeting onto Mr. Nelson's desk. Mr. Nelson thanked him and hung it up for everyone to see. "Since it is a new rule, we will give Daniel another chance. You may sit down, Daniel," he said.

Daniel's bolder cousins grumbled good-naturedly. But Mr. Nelson prevailed.

After a while, class resumed. Their history lesson came not from a book but from Mr. Nelson's knowledge of the antislavery movement leading up to the War Between the States.

Daniel raised his hand.

"Yes, Daniel?" Mr. Nelson called on him.

"You know Anna's mom, Hattie? When she was a girl, her parents helped runaway slaves on their way to freedom."

"I had heard as much. Thank you, Daniel. Where is Anna, by the way?"

While Daniel explained about her having a cold, Jack's arm shot into the air.

"Yes, Jack?" said Mr. Nelson.

"Once, Hattie traded shoes with a slave and got chased by bloodhounds."

Jack finished the story Daniel would have told if Mr. Nelson hadn't sidetracked him, asking about Anna. Great-Uncle Jack, for whom Jack had been named, had been at Hattie's parents' farm along with Grampa Silas and some younger Tandy brothers, gathering cattle for a cattle drive, when Hattie traded shoes with the runaway slave girl.

Mr. Nelson told them about some men who nailed a slave friend into a box in the South and shipped him north to freedom. He said some people along the way knew about it. At each stop, if they could, they gave the man food and water through a hole in the box.

It was snowing when it came time for afternoon recess. The geography game resumed. Daniel's schoolmates added to the nose-to-the-board rule: Anyone who called out the wrong answer had to put his nose to the board.

At Jack's suggestion, the "wrong answer" people

crowded behind the map. The boys got careless with their answers just for the fun of ducking behind the map. Daniel went behind the map. Jack soon followed. "I've got an idea," whispered Jack.

"What?" asked Daniel.

"I'll build a box and mail you to South Dakota."

"It takes five days to get there," said Daniel.

"So? That's less than a week."

"In a box?" exclaimed Daniel. "No thanks! I'll save and buy a ticket."

"Where's the fun in that?" said Jack.

The snow tapered off later in the afternoon. Jack had also come by pony. He and Daniel cut through the woods and detoured past Earl's syrup camp on the way to Daniel's house. The buckets they had put out were empty. It was too cold for the sap to run.

Gram was in the kitchen with Hattie when the boys got home. She invited Jack to join Daniel for milk and pineapple upside-down cake. Daniel and Jack were chasing down the last crumbs and telling Hattie about using her for a clue in the geography game, when someone knocked at the back door. Hattie went to answer it. Daniel recognized Chaldea's voice. His belly flared the way coals will when a log is thrown on the fire.

"What's the matter?" asked Jack.

Daniel jerked a thumb toward the summer porch.

Jack's blue eyes bugged wide. He grabbed his coat and boots and lunged for the back stairs. Daniel slid out of his chair. But Hattie caught him with her remember-your-manners voice:

"Daniel? Miss Jennings has brought Uncle Silas a tonic. And on a day fit neither for man nor beast," she said, all zealous with praise as she ushered Chaldea inside.

Daniel shuffled his feet and chewed his shirt cuff.

"Isn't there something you want to say?" prompted Hattie.

"Sorry about the whistle."

"I thought you said it was the other boy," Chaldea's voice thrashed like noisy birds in brush.

Daniel cringed and bolted for the stairs before Hattie could stop him. *Don't let him be up there, don't let him be up there,* he prayed all the way up.

The sewing room was empty. But there was a damp trail of melting footprints across the floor. Daniel followed it to the landing and down the main staircase to the front hall.

He flung the door wide just as Jack reached the mounting block at the edge of the yard where he had left his pony. Daniel cupped his hands to his mouth. "Hey, Jack! Where you going?"

Jack threw a leg over his pony and tore away without looking back.

The wind was blowing. Maybe he hadn't heard him call. Or was it just the opposite: *He'd heard too much.*

Chapter Six

Snow fell in the night, enough to keep Daniel home from school. He carried Grampa beef tea in the morning, and sat while Gram stitched at his bedside, making a crazy-quilt lap throw from leftover dressmaking scraps. By supper, Grampa asked for real food. Hattie cooked him cereal.

The next morning, Grampa wanted soup for breakfast.

The doctor got through the snow on Wednesday. He gave Grampa some blue pills.

The sun came out on Thursday. The blue pills helped. Grampa came downstairs and whittled sap spiles by the kitchen stove. Years of wear had dulled the ivory knife handle and shaped it to Grampa's hand. He worked wood with the same ease Gram had with cloth, thread, and needle. Daniel doodled on butcher paper, trying to capture the oneness of hand, knife, and wood.

"Why don't you take these over to the syrup camp and see if Earl's working?" said Grampa.

"Too much snow on the ground," Daniel said, rubbing out a line.

"That may not stop Earl. He's a go-getter." Grampa pushed the soft pulp wood out of the hollow end of a spile. "If you don't show, he's liable to replace you.

He's got plenty of Tandy saplings to choose from."

Like Daniel's school, the neighboring farms were thick with Tandys. Not to mention Matthew and the men at the boardinghouse and Jack's father's hired men. Unwilling to lose earnings earmarked for the west, Daniel donned his outdoor clothes and strapped on snowshoes.

It wasn't far to Earl's syrup camp at the edge of the woods. Snow-covered cords of firewood flanked the deserted camp. On the north end was a dirt ramp and holding tank for sap storage. The tank was elevated on a wooden stand. Below, two big black iron kettles hung from iron tripods. They would hold a lot of sap. But not today. It would have to warm considerably before the trees would flow.

Daniel could see at a glance that Earl had not been here. The snow was undisturbed. He cupped his hands to his nose, filtering the frigid air. Wondering over Jack. Wishing he were on a train bound for South Dakota.

A warm south wind blew in the night. The snow was melting by morning. Daniel saddled Boots and set off over the white prairie. Mr. Nelson was just unlocking the door when he arrived.

Jack came a short time later. He dawdled in the boys' hall with some Tandy cousins until time for class.

Mr. Nelson kept the children in at morning recess. They played the geography game. Jack didn't throw any clues Daniel's way. Or join him for lunch, when the time came. His cold shoulder was as clear as hoofprints in the snow.

The day continued to warm. At recess, everyone pulled on coats and boots and mittens and went outside. Mr. Nelson helped some of the children build a snowman. Jack and the older boys threw snowballs. None came Daniel's way.

He was drawing a snowscape with a stick when he saw Jack slip into the schoolhouse, and started to follow. But one of his Tandy cousins got between him and the door.

"Where do you think you're going, snitch?" he asked.

Daniel left a trail of broken sticks on his way to the pony shed. He fed Boots some oats and stroked her neck until Mr. Nelson rang the bell.

The children lined the stove jacket in snowy mittens. The draft on the stove wasn't adjusted right. The coal smoke mingled with damp wool, stinging Daniel's throat. But the school day was almost over before Mr. Nelson opened a window.

A gust of fresh air blew the United States map off the blackboard. Beneath it was a chalk sketch. It was a duplicate of the birthday card drawing Daniel had given to Mr. Nelson. Except for dinner-plate eyes and cup-handle ears. Scrawled in chalk were the words NATE, NATE, BALD ON THE PATE.

Daniel twitched in his seat. Classmates gaped. Little ones slapped hands to slack-jawed mouths. "Ummmm!" they chorused.

Mr. Nelson turned in his chair. He looked from the map on the floor to the board and then to Daniel. The pine boards groaned as he lumbered to his feet. "School is dismissed. Except for you, Daniel," he said, and crooked one finger. "Come forward, please."

Daniel turned a thumb to his chest.

"Yes, you." Mr. Nelson clasped his meaty hands behind his back, waiting.

Daniel stepped into the aisle.

The older girls filed by him with sniffs and snubs, little ones with downcast eyes. Jack curled his lip. Half a dozen boys followed—Tandy cousins, mostly, with prominent noses, ruddy cheeks, and peeping grins.

"Daniel?" prompted Mr. Nelson.

Daniel made his way to the front.

"Stretch out your hands, please."

Daniel presented them, knuckles up. Mr. Nelson caught his wrist and turned his writing hand over. Daniel looked from the ruler on the desk to the paddle on the wall.

"Turn around, please," said Mr. Nelson.

Daniel braced his sit-upon and turned. The classroom was now empty, except for Jack. He loitered off the boys' hall in afternoon shadow.

"You will go your way, Jack, and close the door behind you."

Jack leaped at Mr. Nelson's rumbling voice. The door thunked. Coal shifted. Dropping coals fizzled in the bowels of the stove. Daniel curled his toes, waiting. Waiting. Waiting. Mr. Nelson was a yard away from the hanging paddle, studying the blackboard. "It's a remarkable likeness, Daniel," he said at length.

It *was* remarkable. Daniel had no idea Jack could copy him that well.

"Speak up, son. Is this your artistry?"

"No, sir," said Daniel.

"Whose, then?"

Daniel pressed his lips together and didn't answer.

Mr. Nelson ran a hand over his hairless head and rubbed the back of his neck. At length, he sighed. "Very well. Erase the board, please."

Daniel did so. With Mr. Nelson's permission, he collected his lunch pail and his wraps from the boys' hall.

Mr. Nelson crossed to the stove and crouched before it, poker in hand. He jabbed and rattled. Ashes and clinkers sifted through the stove grate and fell into the ash pan below. Mr. Nelson shoveled them out and into the bucket. "I'll need a note from your grandparents," he called after Daniel.

Daniel stopped short of the door. "What kind of note, sir?"

"The kind that says you have told them why I kept you after school and that they have taken appropriate measures."

Gram had high expectations from her teaching days, and Grampa was death on disrespect. But Daniel couldn't snitch on Jack. Not again.

"Sir?" he said, and shuffled his feet. "Could I get it from my father instead?" he said finally.

"Is your father home?"

"No. But he'll probably come when he gets my letter,"

said Daniel. "I wrote and told him about Grampa's liver being sick."

"Your grandfather Tandy? I didn't know he was ill."

Daniel nodded. "Dr. Ritter says his blood's doing poorly, too."

"I'm sorry, Daniel. I hadn't heard," said Mr. Nelson.

"If my father doesn't come, he could still write the note, couldn't he?"

"You intend to be honest with him?"

"Yes, sir."

"All right, then. But you are on your honor as a gentleman," said Mr. Nelson. "I'll be awaiting his note."

Daniel left the schoolhouse, braced for Jack. But the school yard was empty except for little Anna. She was waiting on the stiles for Matthew to come pick her up.

Jack's pony was gone from the pony shed. So was Boots.

Daniel climbed up on the roof and shaded his eyes. Tandy cousins and horses stood out against the snow. They turned through the gate at Brock Cemetery, a little southwest of the schoolhouse. Jack was out in front, leading Boots.

Chapter Seven

"Hey, Daniel. You're on the roof!" called Anna. She crossed the snowy yard on turned-in toes, trailing her woolen scarf. "Did Mr. Nelson paddle you?"

"No," said Daniel.

"How come?"

"Because I didn't do it."

Anna stopped below him. She brushed broomstick straw hair out of robin-egg eyes, tipped her dimpled chin, and asked, "Who did?"

"I don't know."

"Jackfrey?" asked Anna.

"Maybe."

"I'll ask him."

"You stay out of it," said Daniel.

"Are *you* going to ask him?"

"No. Where's your dad?"

"McLean. He had to pick up the girls first."

Anna's older sisters had graduated to an upper-level school in McLean, a mile and a half away.

Anna pestered Daniel until he helped her up the tree alongside the pony shed and onto the roof. They made snow angels on the roof, then kicked them to the ground. Anna giggled and said they were flying.

Daniel's Story

Soon, Matthew and the girls came along in a wagon box mounted on sled runners. Daniel climbed in after Anna and nestled in the straw.

They didn't slow again until they reached Matthew's lane at the south edge of the timber. Daniel climbed down, opened the gate for Matthew, and thanked him for the ride.

Grampa Silas's farm was a quarter mile farther along. Once home, Daniel changed out of his school clothes, grabbed a handful of cookies, and tramped to Earl's syrup camp.

Earl had cleared the snow from the woodpiles. Sap was boiling in the black iron kettles. Steam clouds and wafting wood smoke rolled and tumbled skyward as Earl knocked fire down to coals. Daniel grabbed a piece of wood and crouched beside him.

"You just missed the gathering crew. They're collecting on the other side of the creek," said Earl. He laid the wood on the fire and crossed to the pile for more. "Jack said you weren't coming."

"I had to change my clothes," said Daniel.

"How is Uncle Silas?" asked Earl.

"Better, Gram says. Want a cookie?" Daniel offered his last one. "Raisin oatmeal. Hattie made them."

"Thanks."

Earl shoved the cookie in his mouth and crossed to the wooden tank where the gathered sap was stored. It sat higher than the round kettles and lower than the dirt ramp. There was a valve on it. Earl turned it off, stopping the sap flow down a pipe into the nearest kettle. "If you're here to work, empty the buckets on this side of the creek."

Daniel grabbed two gathering pails. The buckets on the south side of the trees were full. He slopped sap down his pant-leg and into his overshoe on the way back to the holding tank. It was stinging cold.

The horse-drawn gathering tank came across the plank bridge spanning Timber Creek. Chains jingled. Sled runners slushed over the melting snow. The man handling the lines swung the team in line with the ramp. Jack was riding on the sled with the wooden gathering tub. He jumped off as the horses climbed the ramp.

There was a pipe arm on the gathering tub. The hired man lowered the arm and slipped a gutter-shaped piece of tin beneath it.

"Watch it empty," he told Jack, then ambled over to talk to Earl.

Gravity channeled the sap from the gathering barrel down the gutter into the holding tank.

Daniel was climbing the ramp with his buckets of sap when Jack turned and saw him. Jack thrust his chin in the air. "What're *you* doing here?"

"Working for Earl." Daniel set the heavy buckets down and squared his jaw, too. "Where's Boots?"

"How should I know?"

"You took him."

"Because you told on me to Chaldea."

"I didn't mean to."

"Doesn't matter, you're still a tattler."

Daniel's Story

"No worse than a sneak," claimed Daniel.

"Who you calling a sneak?"

"You. Drawing that picture like mine so Mr. Nelson would think it was me."

"Suppose you squealed on me for that, too."

"What if I did?"

"Then you can quit calling yourself a Tandy. The boys and I had a meeting after school. That's what we decided," said Jack.

"It isn't up to you."

"Sure it is. Grampa Jack and the others let Uncle Silas be a Tandy, as long as he acted like one. Same goes for you." Jack narrowed his eyes. "So, did you tell?"

Daniel gripped one of the buckets by the handle and stepped around him.

"*Did* you?" Jack knocked into him with his shoulder.

Daniel slid in the muddy snow and fell with the bucket of sap. The icy chill brought him shouting to his feet. He flew at Jack. Jack fell backward against the gathering tank. The startled team lurched down the ramp. The hired man bolted after the spurting tank and two-ton team. Earl came after Daniel and Jack.

"You're spilling my sap! Clear out, both of you!" he shouted.

Sap squished in Daniel's boots as he leaped away. Jack bolted away, too. "Sorehead!" he hollered.

"You shoved first!"

"I was talking to Earl." Jack wiggled his finger in one

ear, turning slush to a smear. "You'd have thought it was blood we spilled."

"His," agreed Daniel.

The quirk at the corner of Jack's mouth widened into a grin. Daniel's mouth twitched, too. He relaxed his balled fists.

"You have cow chips in your teeth," claimed Jack.

"Huh-uh."

"Mud, then."

Daniel sucked his teeth. "It's raisin. Hattie made cookies."

"Got any?"

"Not with me."

"What kind?" asked Jack.

"Raisin, I just said."

"My favorite," said Jack. "I'll race you."

Daniel thought he meant on foot. But when they reached the edge of the woods, there was Boots huddled with Jack's pony.

"So did you tell on me or didn't you?" Jack asked as they mounted up.

"Tandys don't tell on Tandys, remember?"

Jack blinked his eyes and bunched his windburned cheeks. "What about with Chaldea?"

"I couldn't help it. She hexed me," claimed Daniel. "Thanks to you."

"We're even, then," said Jack. "So when did you want to start building the box?"

"What box?"

Daniel's Story

"The one for you to go visit your dad."

"I told you, I'm getting a ticket," said Daniel.

"How?" asked Jack. "You got us fired."

Daniel had no idea how. But he would go. He *would* and no one could stop him.

Chapter Eight

Dad?

It's me, Daniel. I got in trouble because of a picture Jack drew on the board. But Tandys can't tell on Tandys. Grampa's better.
Mr. Nelson wants a letter saying I told you why he kept me after school. I helped gather sap for Earl. Jack and me spilled some. But not on purpose.

Your son, Daniel.

Daniel left out the part about being fired. He didn't tell his grandparents, either. Or Hattie, when she came the next morning.

"Matthew is going to work for Earl today," Hattie said as she shook the ashes from the cookstove. "He's taking the girls to school first. I told Anna she could ride home with you."

"All right," Daniel said, rubbing the sleep from his eyes.

"Don't forget and leave her, now. I'm counting on you," added Hattie.

And he'd been counting on syrup work. Daniel

brought his overshoes in from the summer porch. He stood over the ash bucket, scraping off the mud with a table knife and wishing for another chance.

After breakfast, Daniel hurried to school to talk it over with Jack. But Jack didn't come. It was unusual for him to miss school. It made the day long. At the end of it, Anna climbed up on Boots behind Daniel. She hung on tight and chattered all the way home about her sisters getting to spend the night at Matthew's sister's home in McLean.

Grampa was in the kitchen, pale and unshaven. His creaking chair and chipping knife harmonized with Hattie's rolling pin as she rolled out pie dough at the table. Daniel closed the door behind him.

"There's the little worker," said Grampa. "The sap's running. Change your clothes and go on over to the camp. Don't keep Earl waiting."

Daniel tugged at his coat cuffs. "Grampa?"

Curled shavings stopped flying. Grampa lifted his knobby chin.

Daniel couldn't think how to tell him what had happened. "What does a train ticket cost?" he asked instead.

"To South Dakota? We've had this conversation, son. Anyway, those tracks run both ways," added Grampa.

"You wouldn't know it, no more often than Pierce comes home," inserted Hattie. She brushed flour from her hands. "What's it been—four years?"

"Don't you start, too," said Grampa. He urged Daniel toward the back stairs with a sweep of his pocketknife.

Daniel paused on the stairs just out of view.

"Poor thing," murmured Hattie. "All he wants is to see his dad."

"He can't go alone," replied Grampa. "And I'm in no shape for five days on the train."

"I'll go with him," said Anna. "Can I, Mama?"

Daniel rolled his eyes and trudged up the stairs. He opened his unmailed letter and added a postscript:

P.S. Dad, if you can't come see us, I can come see you. All I need is a train ticket.

Daniel put the letter in his pocket and went downstairs again.

Anna looked up from sprinkling ground cinnamon and sugar over pie dough scraps. "Wait for me!" she cried as Daniel pulled on his coat.

"I'm only going to the st—syrup camp."

"I want to help Earl, too. Please, Mama?" urged Anna.

"If you want to help, help me," said Hattie. "Line up the dining room chairs. You can play train while I finish this pie. Then I'll bring the furniture wax."

Daniel posted his letter at the store and came out to find the sun had slipped behind the clouds. He turned Boots back the way they had come, over the crossing and into the trees. Every maple tree he passed was dripping sap. But with Matthew working for him, it seemed unlikely Earl would need him.

Just as well go home, admit what had happened, and let Anna coax him into playing train. It was a favorite game of hers, and more entertaining than shivering and wishing he could get his job back.

Daniel couldn't see the camp for the creek and the trees in between. But the faint scent of maple wafted on the breeze, and steam clouds sailed overhead. The wind stung his cheeks and made his eyes drip as he lingered, trying to make up his mind. At length, he urged Boots onto the narrow bridge leading over the creek and onto the camp.

Earl was stirring the kettle with a long-handled wooden paddle. He motioned to Daniel. "Fire's burning down. Dig down in that pile and find me some dry logs, would you?"

Daniel blinked. Recovering from his surprise, he bailed off his pony, gathered an armload of dry wood, and dropped it at Earl's feet. "Anything else?"

"Empty the buckets here around the camp. When Matthew returns with the sap tub, you can go with him. And don't spill the sap!" he called after Daniel.

It wasn't long before Matthew came with the sap sled and team. Jack was with him. He jumped off the sled and threw a snowball at Daniel.

Daniel ducked. "I thought you were sick," he called.

"Nope. Trees ran all night. Earl needed help."

"I guess we aren't fired after all," said Daniel.

Jack shrugged. "Earl doesn't have to pay us what he pays men."

When Matthew had dumped his load, Daniel and Jack climbed up on the sled with the wooden gathering tank and rode back to the crossing.

The man who had been driving the team yesterday came out of Walker's Store and joined them. They turned north to collect in a section of woods alongside the railroad tracks.

Matthew and the hired man talked about horse races, politics, and cheap land in Oklahoma. Jack talked about his aching legs and cold feet. Daniel didn't talk at all. He tramped from tree to gathering sled to tree and back again, trying not to spill sap. Or count his chickens before they hatched.

It was dark by the time Daniel got home. He peeled off his wet clothes, washed, ate supper, and tumbled into bed to daydream about going west. But he was so tired, his eyes closed even before the train left the station.

It set a pattern for the days to come, days so full that Daniel sometimes forgot to watch the mail for the note he needed from his father.

One Saturday near the end of March, when the ground was dry and the sun was shining, Grampa went with Daniel to the syrup camp. He pulled up a crate and kept Earl company while Daniel went to the woods with the gathering crew.

That evening, over supper, Grampa told of his boyhood days when maple sugar was the standard sweetener on the prairie.

Daniel's Story

"It has been years since we've had maple candy," said Gram.

"We'll make some, shall we, Daniel?" said Grampa. "It's hard to top," he added, closing his eyes as if savoring the taste. A moment later, he was snoring.

Gram took the shawl from her shoulders, circled the table, and covered Grampa with it. Daniel thought it would wake him. But it didn't. His chin settled into his chest. His hair fell across his forehead in thin white strands. His ashen lips puttered with each breath.

"He's all right, isn't he?" asked Daniel.

"For a man his age," said Gram. She thumped past on her cane, and sat down again. But she didn't finish her pie, and her tea grew cold, untouched.

Daniel carried his empty plate to the sink and Gram's words upstairs to bed. He cradled his pillow beneath the covers but couldn't get comfortable. His legs twitched. His arms ached. He rubbed his eyes and said his prayers.

Maybe he wouldn't stay the whole summer with his father.

Maybe just a few weeks.

He would sketch lots of pictures of Indians and stuff and bring them home to Grampa.

✳ 51 ✳

Chapter Nine

At the end of March, the weather warmed and the sap stopped flowing. Earl paid Daniel off in maple syrup. Daniel sold two gallons to Mr. Walker at the store, who put it into smaller containers for resale. Grampa Silas bought Daniel's remaining syrup with plans to make candy. But he had another spell with his liver late in April. Daniel wrote his father again in early May.

Dad?

It's me, Daniel. Syrup season is over. I saved my money. It's a surprise. You'll see. Miss Jennings comes to the house with her remedies. That was her, fell off her bicycle. The picture I sent. Jack says she talks to the dead and they answer. He can't say it in front of Hattie. Or mention Oklahoma Territory. Matthew's wanting land there, but Hattie says the government gave it to Indians and it isn't likely they're a bit happier about giving it back than the Sioux out your way.
I hope you didn't forget my note. I gave Mr. Nelson my word.

Your son, Daniel
P. S. Grampa's liver complains again. He's cross.

Absentminded, too. It was little things. Like misplacing his reading glasses and shaving mug and putting his pocketknife in the kitchen drawer along with the silverware.

One morning as the school year neared an end, Hattie fixed pancakes. Syrup on the table reminded Grampa about making candy. When Daniel came home that afternoon, sweet maple scents wafted in the air. Grampa motioned to him with a long-handled spoon. "You're just in time to stir."

Daniel crossed to his side and peered into the pan of boiling syrup. "What do we do?"

"It'll have to boil awhile longer, then cool," said Grampa. "Have you seen my pocketknife?"

"It's mixed in with the silver."

"Can't anybody leave anything alone?" Grampa collected his pocketknife and turned away.

"Where are you going?" asked Daniel.

"Upstairs."

"What about the candy?"

"Keep stirring and don't let it boil over on Hattie's stove," said Grampa.

"Where is Hattie, anyway?"

"She went home early with a headache. Had Indian Territory written all over it. That reminds me—there's a letter for you on the table."

Daniel's heart jumped at the familiar handwriting. He tore open the envelope.

Dear Daniel,

I'm sorry to be so long in writing. I've been away, hauling goods to the Black Hills.

Earl has grown into an enterprising fellow, by the sound of it. You made me curious. I hope your surprise is maple-flavored.

I hung your drawings with the others. They brighten the cabin walls.

I suppose it is the cheap land interesting Matthew. But I doubt if he can talk Hattie into pulling up roots.

Regarding your trouble at school, I don't see how word from me will resolve anything. But I have enclosed a letter for your teacher, as you asked. Give my love to Father and Harmony. I'll write them soon.

Pierce

Daniel hoped he was right about Hattie.

The note to Mr. Nelson was sealed in an enclosed envelope. He held it up to the light, then turned back to the stove and waved the letter over the rising steam.

"What's your father have to say?" Grampa called through the ceiling grate.

Daniel's pulse gave a guilty leap.

"Daniel?"

"I'm stirring. He says he'll write you soon."

"I won't hold my breath," said Grampa. "Is your arm getting tired?"

"A little," said Daniel.

"I'm coming."

Daniel tucked his father's letter to Mr. Nelson under the tablecloth.

"We'll test it," Grampa said, joining Daniel in the kitchen.

He pumped a shallow dish of water at the sink and brought it to the stove. "Drizzle a little syrup in there. That's it. Let it cool a second. Now reach in, see if you can push it into a ball."

Daniel dived his fingers into the cold water. The syrup was warm and tacky. He rolled it into a soft glob.

"Does it hold together?"

"Just about." Daniel popped it into his mouth and licked his fingers. It dissolved sweet and gummy on his tongue. "Yum."

Grampa crossed to the grate and cupped his hands to his mouth. "Harmony?"

"Have you tested it?" Gram called back.

"Yes. But we're open to a second opinion," replied Grampa.

"I'll be right there."

Gram thumped down the stairs on her cane and repeated Grampa's cold-water test. "Perfect," she said. "Set it off the stove. I'm going to sit on the porch while it cools. Get my quilt for me, would you, Daniel?"

The quilt was made of blocks sewn from inch-wide satin strips. The strips stacked together so that each block resembled a log cabin. The fabrics Gram had used were from ribbons and fancy outgrown garments.

Some had been cut from dresses Daniel's mother had once worn.

On his way through the kitchen, Daniel reassured himself his letter was still beneath the rumpled tablecloth, then joined his grandparents on the summer porch.

"Who is this one for, Gram?" Daniel asked as he dropped the quilt in her lap.

"You can keep it if you like," said Gram. "Or we can send it to your father."

"A Log Cabin quilt for his log cabin house," said Grampa.

Daniel stroked his face with one corner of the quilt. "Slippery."

Gram smiled and patted his cheek. "More showy than practical, perhaps."

Grampa leaned forward in his chair, looking across the yard to the log cabin toolshed. "The first winter I spent in that old cabin, I thought I'd freeze to death. I hear the wind really howls in South Dakota."

"I planned to make red center squares to represent home fires burning. But Hattie suggested white," continued Gram.

"I don't know why that boy can't come home and farm like his brothers." Grampa followed his own train of thoughts.

"The white is leftover scraps from the christening gown your mother made for you. See, Daniel?" Gram said, pointing out a white center square no bigger than the end of Daniel's finger.

"Or he could clear out the tools and fix the cabin

roof, if he's so partial to primitive living." Grampa nudged Gram. "What do you think?"

"I think you ought to push the eyesore in and quit beating dead horses," replied Gram.

"Humph!" Grampa unfolded his pocketknife. He whittled a stick to a fine point while Gram bound the edges of the quilt.

Daniel blew on a little hillock of whittling shavings, trying to make up his mind about the quilt. It was a pretty thing, even if it didn't hold any memories for him. "I guess Dad should have it," he said finally. "Can we send him some candy, too?"

"That's a nice idea," said Gram.

"You'd better wait to see how it turns out," advised Grampa. "And leave some for me to take to town with me tomorrow."

"You're going to Bloomington?" said Gram.

"Yes. Do you have a list?"

"No, but I'll make one," replied Gram. "I'd like a bicycle while you're there."

"A bicycle?" Grampa crooked a white eyebrow. "With a barn full of horses?"

"Bicycles don't bolt at train whistles. They don't have to be fed, groomed, or harnessed. And they stay where you put them," reasoned Gram.

"Folks will say you've thrown in with Miss Jennings," Grampa said with a sidelong glance. "Are you going to pedal about with a remedy basket, too?"

"A basket *would* be nice," Gram said, matching his inflection. "You can put that on your list."

"What makes you think you can ride the thing?"

"I'll help you learn, Gram," said Daniel.

"Go see if that pan is cool enough to touch, and quit interrupting your elders," said Grampa.

Daniel ambled into the kitchen, glanced back over his shoulder, then slipped his father's note to Mr. Nelson from beneath the tablecloth. He tugged at the loosened seal, slipped a thin slip of paper out of the envelope, and stole up the stairs.

Chapter Ten

Dear Mr. Nelson,

Daniel tells me you kept him after school. I'm unclear on the circumstances, but if I understand correctly, Daniel is covering up for his cousin Jack. Daniel appears to be satisfied with matters as they stand. I'm not sure it's fair to Jack. But I'll leave that to you.

Pierce Tandy

Daniel's heart plummeted. To pass this letter along would only invite more trouble! He crammed it back into the envelope. What was he supposed to do now? And what did his father mean, "I'm not sure it's fair to Jack"?

Daniel hid the letter in the Pony Express saddlebag, then bolted down the stairs again to find Grampa stirring the thickened syrup. It had lost its amber shine and turned the color of cream and was as thick as wallpaper paste.

"Pour it. Quickly, before it sets!" urged Gram.

Daniel and Grampa scrambled like ants, scraping the contents into cake pans. In moments, it was firm.

When it had cooled, Gram cut it into squares.

"Perfect!" Grampa said, urging a piece on Daniel.

It melted in his mouth, creamy sweet and hard to resist. Daniel nibbled and nibbled and nibbled, his father's letter to Mr. Nelson all the while nibbling at him. In his place, what would Jack do?

He wouldn't give the teacher a tattling letter, that's what he *wouldn't* do. Jack would come up with a brainstorm. *Think like Jack, that's the trick.*

The more Daniel thought, the more he nibbled. By bedtime, he had a headache, a stomachache, and an idea. He decided to sleep on it. Maybe something better would come to him in the night.

Nothing did. He crawled out of bed at sunup and stumbled to the window, with pencil, paper, and letter in hand. He put a sheet of paper over his father's letter and held both to the window. His father's handwriting came through the thin foolscap. Carefully, he traced chosen words and phrases and, in so doing, composed a note in his father's hand:

Dear Sir,

Daniel tells me that you kept him after school. I'm satisfied with matters as they stand.

Pierce Tandy

It looked too short. Daniel chewed the shirt cuff of his long-handle underwear and studied his father's note.

Daniel's Story

He tried again:

Dear Sir,

Daniel tells me that you kept him after school. I under-stand. On the circumstances, it's clear you were fair. I'm satisfied with matters as they stand.

Pierce Tandy

Better. But still too short.

Hattie tapped on the talking tube. "Daniel? Are you dressed? Hurry, or you'll be late for school."

Mr. Nelson had waited for several months. What was one more day? Daniel shoved the papers into the Pony Express saddlebag, dressed for school, and hurried downstairs to breakfast.

Hattie packed two pieces of maple candy into his lunch bucket.

Jack talked him into sharing one piece at noon and the other after school on their way to the store where Jack was to fill a list for his mother. They rode north past fields of sprouting corn and into the trees of Funks Grove.

There was a train stopped on the tracks. A crowd milled near the crossing. As they approached on their ponies, Earl turned and hurried toward them on a choppy stride. His eyes were wide, his mouth taut and ridged in white. He waved them back. "You boys go home."

Startled, Daniel reined in Boots.

"Mama said go to the store. See? I've got a list." Jack

pulled it from his shirt pocket and urged his pony forward. "Flour, tea, thread—"

Earl snatched the list from Jack's hand.

Jack rose in the stirrups, trying to see past the crowd. "What's all these people? What're they looking at?"

"Go on home, Jackfrey. Send Father. Go, now!"

Earl grabbed the halter, led Jack's pony around, and slapped it on the rump. Daniel followed on Boots. It was a short gallop to the edge of the woods, where Daniel left Jack and crossed the open pasture.

Chaldea's bicycle was cast to one side by the summer porch. She was in the kitchen with her hair in knots and no sign of her basket of remedies.

"I thought you should know before they brought him to the house," Daniel heard Chaldea say.

Gram sank into a chair with a moan. The room shrank as Chaldea edged past him and out the door.

"Where's Grampa?" he asked when she had gone.

Gram was too full of tears to say. Daniel lunged for the stairs.

Hattie sat midway up, weeping. "It's Uncle Silas. He stepped out in front of a train." Sobbing, she gathered Daniel in. She kept her arms around him, down the stairs and to the table and Gram. They talked in spurts. Like floating sticks in choked streams.

The word "dead" was not spoken. But the certainty of it hovered over Daniel as the boardinghouse men filed in from the fields and stood in silent clusters, hats in hand.

There was a pebble on the step. The kind that made scratches. Small, hard, sharp. It was ordinary. Of no interest. Daniel fixed his eye on it the way a plowboy will a post so as to keep his furrow straight.

Gram and Grampa's sons trailed in from nearby farms with wet faces and broken voices. A wire was sent to their sisters, all of them married and living in Bloomington.

Neighbors and friends and family came until the house was overflowing. With each new face, Gram went over it again:

"He had business in town. But he didn't feel well this morning. He decided to wait for the afternoon train."

She dabbed her swollen eyes and scarred cheeks and plunged ahead, repeating what she had heard from Chaldea—what had now been confirmed by others with firsthand accounts of the accident.

"Maralee saw him look. But he must have mistaken it for the local train."

The train that hit Grampa wasn't the local. It was a through train. It was hurtling along at thirty miles an hour and could not stop. The pilot beam had thrown Daniel's grandfather into a keg of railroad spikes.

Again and again, Daniel heard it. He listened hard each time. As if in the retelling Gram could find a new detail that would change the outcome. Then they brought Grampa's body home.

A heaviness scorched Daniel's eyes and throat and tightened the knot in his belly. He slipped off to the woods and tossed rocks in the creek, thinking about the crossing. The sun was sinking by the time he reached it.

Everyone had gone. There was nothing to see except the broken keg of spikes and a familiar basket on the bench beneath a hickory tree. Daniel lifted the napkin covering it. Inside was melted maple candy.

Later, he learned that Grampa had left the basket and crossed the tracks to chat with a workman in the seed house where corn was stored. That he heard the whistle and bade the fellow good-bye, saying that he had to collect his basket before boarding the train for Bloomington.

The workman thought it was the local train, too. Until the last moment, when he noticed its speed and shouted a warning. But he could not outshout the oncoming train.

A telegram was sent to Daniel's father. Daniel sent him a letter, too.

Dad,

It's me, Daniel. You heard about Grampa by now. Hattie says it's too far for you to get here in time for the funeral. But maybe you'll come, anyway.

Your son, Daniel

The next day, on his way to mail the letter, Daniel saw a small wooden cross driven into the ground near the spot where the train had struck Grampa.

It was just a few feet from where Chaldea had wrecked her bicycle the day Jack had blown the whistle.

Chapter Eleven

The wake passed in a blur of company, covered dishes, and conversation. Grampa would have enjoyed the gathering. Especially the remembering. He would have liked the funeral, too, if he could have heard the nice things his friends and family said about him.

The preacher talked in his sermon about the Lord coming back to restore all things, including dead people. It was the sort of sermon, when Daniel was very small, that had made him hope for a good, hard rain to wash his mother up and his father home.

Grampa's sons and nephews carried the casket to the cemetery beside the white-frame church. Folks gathered around the grave, Gram flanked by grown-up children. Daniel looked around for Hattie. She had one arm encircling Anna. The other she opened to him and pulled him to her side.

"'Behold, I shew you a mystery,'" said the minister. "'We shall not all sleep, but we shall all be changed. In a moment, in the twinkling of an eye, at the last trump: for the trumpet shall sound, and the dead shall be raised incorruptible, and we shall all be changed.'"

Bible pages fluttered in the breeze as the pastor lifted his face to the clouds. "'O death, where is thy sting?'" he asked. "'O grave, where is thy victory?'"

The sting was in Daniel's churning gut and burning eyes. Hattie pressed a handkerchief into his hand. He wiped his dripping nose and smelled sage.

Across the open grave stood Chaldea, her hexing fingers in faded black gloves.

After the funeral, everyone went home, and Daniel returned to school. A week later, Mr. Nelson passed him to the next level with no mention of the promised letter from his father or his "honor as a gentleman."

Daniel rode home past thriving fields and ripening wheat. Hattie was waiting for him in the kitchen. "There's someone here to see you," she said, and nudged him toward the parlor.

A man in a stiff-bosomed shirt rose from a side chair. His hair trailed past his weathered neck, dark against his high white collar. It was the mole at one corner of his mouth that settled it for Daniel. That, and the way he carried himself. *Like Grampa, before he got sick.* Heat rose behind Daniel's eyes. "I was away hauling freight when word came," said his father.

"I thought you weren't coming."

By letter, Daniel knew him. In person, he was a stranger. He couldn't say "Dad." And "Father" didn't fit, either. He shifted his feet as his father picked up a drawing from Gram's rosewood center table. It was of Anna. Daniel had sketched her collecting tickets from make-believe passengers on her train of dining room chairs.

"One of Hattie's girls?" Pierce asked.

Daniel nodded.

His father studied it a moment longer, then leaned it against Gram's porcelain clock. His gaze flicked back to Daniel. "Look at you, half grown."

Daniel rubbed the Oriental carpet with the toe of his shoe.

"How are you getting along?"

"Okay, I guess," murmured Daniel. He tucked his hand in his pocket and closed his fingers around Grampa's pocketknife. He had found it in the silverware drawer the morning of the funeral. "Where's Gram?" he asked into the silence.

"Upstairs, resting. The doctor was here earlier."

"She's having trouble sleeping. He gave her something to help," said Hattie. She bustled into the parlor, set a silver tray of iced cakes and beverages on the center table, and slipped her arm around Daniel. "How was your last day of school?"

"Mr. Nelson gave us oranges and peppermint sticks."

"Then I guess there's no danger of spoiling your appetite. Coffee, tea, or milk, Pierce?"

"Coffee's fine," said Pierce. He sat down on Gram's Moorish divan.

Daniel perched on an embroidered armchair. He eyed the fine porcelain cups and Washington tumblers as Hattie poured. "Are we having company?"

"Not today. We'll get the whole family together while your father's here, though."

"Don't go to a lot of trouble, Hattie," said Pierce.

"Nonsense," Hattie said, joining him on the divan. "You'll want to see everyone while you're home. The boardinghouse cook is going to help with the meal, provided we can find someone to cook for the workmen. I thought I'd check with Maralee. You remember Maralee, don't you? Maralee Jennings?"

Daniel's father repeated the name. "Is she the one you pelted with green apples on the way to the mill that time?"

"No, that was Dora June Carlson," said Hattie. "And I didn't pelt her. I couldn't. You took my apples."

Daniel ate his cake and drank his milk and listened as Hattie and his father recalled their childhood days. It was like watching Gram's hands move over quilts, recollecting the garments from which they had been cut.

When the refreshments were gone, Daniel went upstairs to his room. His father followed with gifts from the west. There was a bone whistle decorated with porcupine quills, and a toy horse made of wood. The horse had real hair for a mane and tail. The legs were delicately carved—the front ones bent, the back ones fully extended.

Daniel fingered the flared nostrils and open mouth. "It's good."

"Isn't it?"

There was no mistaking the pride in his father's voice. Daniel asked, "Did you make it?"

"No." Pierce peeled back brown paper from a doll made of buckskin. "This is the rider."

The doll had long hair and a painted face. He wore a scrap of cotton for a shirt, cotton trousers, a tiny feather in his hair, deerskin shoes, and a blanket about his shoulders.

"Fifty-fifty clothes," said his father.

Puzzled, Daniel lifted his face.

"Mixing traditional Indian apparel with store-bought clothes," his father explained.

Daniel thanked him for the horse and rider. He showed him the peg Grampa had driven into the wall to display the Pony Express saddlebag.

"He liked it, did he?" Pierce said, seeming pleased.

Daniel nodded. "He said you weren't much older than me when you carried the mail across Indian Territory."

"Sixteen," Pierce said, smiling. "Even then, it was plain I wasn't a blood Tandy. Must have gotten the itchy feet from old Grampa Pierce."

Daniel knew a little about Grampa Silas's father, Boyce Pierce. He was a soldier and, like Daniel's father's, his feet had "itched" to travel. When Grampa Silas was a young boy, Boyce died of a snakebite. His mother, Julia, married a Tandy, and Grampa Silas took the name.

"Did you get homesick when you ran away from home?" asked Daniel.

"Did I!" His father smiled. "I can't tell you how I yearned for green grass and timber and rich, black dirt."

Daniel crossed to the wall peg and put the carved horse and doll inside. His father followed, bringing the whistle. "It's made of eagle bone. The Sioux used them in the Sun Dance," he explained.

"You've seen them dance the Sun Dance?"

"Some time ago. The government has since put a stop to it."

"Why?" asked Daniel.

"Dancing Indians make non-Indians edgy. Even when the dance is a prayer."

"What kind of a prayer?"

"Any and every kind," said his father. "A petition for good hunting. For a sick relative. For a woman's heart. For strong medicine against an adversary."

Daniel eyelids twitched. "Can a dance be a hex?"

"You mean put a curse on someone?" asked Pierce.

"Cause bad things to happen," Daniel said, nodding.

"Why? Is your heart bad toward someone?"

"No, not mine." Losing courage, Daniel let it drop without mentioning his fears concerning Chaldea and the part he and Jack may have played in Grampa's death.

Chapter Twelve

Gram slept until dinnertime and awoke with a headache. She asked Hattie if she would mind staying through supper. Hattie sent Daniel to the barn, where the men were doing chores. One of them agreed to take a message to Hattie's family that she would be late coming home.

Pierce sat in Grampa's chair at the head of the table. Hattie served, then sat down beside Gram across the table from Daniel. After the blessing, Pierce thanked Gram for the Log Cabin quilt.

"You got it, then?" said Gram.

"The candy, too?" asked Daniel.

"Yes."

"Was it melted?" asked Gram.

"No," said Pierce.

"Grampa and I made it."

"It was very good," said his father.

Pleased, Daniel unfolded Grampa's pocketknife from his pocket and cut his meat with it.

"Use your table knife, please, Daniel," Gram corrected his manners in her "company" voice.

Daniel supposed that meant his father was company. He tore a piece of bread in two, folded it over Grampa's knife, and nicked himself, rubbing the blade clean.

"I was alarmed to see in the papers where folks out your way are returning east for fear of the Indians," Gram said as Daniel sucked the smear of blood from his thumb.

"Things have been ticklish ever since the breakup of the Great Sioux Reservation," Daniel's father replied.

"Silas was well read on the subject," said Gram. "He felt the government was generous in their dealings."

"I can see how he would," said Pierce, "but land ownership is a new concept to the Sioux."

"Every Indian family *did* get a farm, didn't they? Before the land was ceded for settlement?" asked Hattie.

"The opportunity was there. For those who touched the feather." At Gram's puzzled glance, Pierce added, "Signed the agreement."

"Manifest Destiny," Gram said, her face clearing. "Your father believed in it firmly."

"Yes. I remember," said Daniel's father. "'Kingdoms rise and kingdoms fall.'"

A fresh blood droplet had pooled on the pad of Daniel's thumb. He looked up to see Hattie watching him, lips pursed. He stopped sucking his thumb and glanced at his father, who was still talking about the Indians.

"The buffalo are all but gone, and with them, a whole way of living," said Pierce. "Reservation life is pretty dull by comparison. The Sioux are mistrustful of the homesteaders who are crowding in. The feeling is mutual. Most homesteaders are ignorant of Indian ways and fearful, particularly of those who openly resent the loss of their land and grieve for the old red road."

Daniel's Story

Daniel looked up from wrapping his linen napkin around his thumb. "I didn't know Indians had roads. I thought all they used were game trails and warpaths."

"'The old red road' means their way of living before white men came," explained Pierce. "The hunting and feasting and sacred ceremonies. Warfare, too."

"I shouldn't think they would miss that part," murmured Hattie.

"Oh, but they do. They have always known how to die bravely. Living with their losses is the challenge now. They're left with a hole in their spirit."

"I should think the missionaries would have taught them how to fill that hole," said Hattie.

"The missionaries work hard meeting needs through the churches and schools they've established," said Pierce. "Some among the Sioux have grasped that bond of brotherhood and converted to Christianity. Others combine it with their own beliefs while still others give it a uniquely Indian slant. Take Wovoka, for example. He's a Piute prophet telling anyone who will listen that the Messiah is going to return next spring as an Indian."

Hattie's eyes widened. "You don't mean Jesus?"

"According to Wovoka," Pierce replied, nodding. "He's teaching his followers songs and a dance they're calling the Messiah Dance. He's saying those who embrace his teachings and dance will be caught up in the air while the Messiah makes the earth new again."

"How's He going to do that?" asked Daniel.

"With waves of new dirt. That's what Wovoka is preaching, anyway," said Pierce.

Daniel visualized dirt falling like rain, lapping at trees and houses the way the creek did when it got out of its banks.

"Those who dance are supposed to be dropped gently to the restored earth, where they can walk the old red road with their loved ones returned from the happy hunting ground."

"Ghosts?" Daniel said, intrigued.

"Some are calling it the Ghost Dance religion. But if I have it right, Wovoka isn't preaching ghosts. He's talking about the dead rising to live again."

"That's scriptural," inserted Hattie. "The Bible says the dead will be raised to life at Jesus's second coming. However, it also says that no man knows the day or the hour when He will return. Wovoka sounds like a false prophet to me."

"Last fall, the Sioux sent a delegation to meet him and check out his claims," said Pierce. "I look forward to hearing their impressions."

Gram put her fork down and twisted her wedding band. "You don't have to go back, Pierce. You can stay and farm. It was always your father's wish."

"I know that, Harmony. And thank you," said Pierce. "But I can't stay. Not with things so uneasy at home."

"Home." The word broke in Daniel's ears like glass in a dark room. Ghost Dance religion and pricked thumb forgotten, he pushed peas into his potatoes. Watched the dam break and the gravy spill.

Chapter Thirteen

Daniel's father stayed six days. It wasn't like in Daniel's daydreams: They didn't go to the field together. His father didn't tell him stories about his mother, or look to some future time when they might share a home.

The only home his father spoke of was in the west. A breeze could turn his thoughts that way. He would talk of open sky and bitter winters and summer's heat. Of the stark, hushed Badlands. Of ore that had brought greed and vice and violence to the mysterious Black Hills so sacred to the Sioux. And of the Sioux themselves and their factions and conflicts and hardships.

If it's so hard, wondered Daniel, *why does he stay?*

It was if he had "touched the feather" in a one-sided treaty giving himself to that distant land. And something else. Daniel wasn't sure what—just that it was strong.

On the last day of his visit, the whole Tandy clan came to Gram's. They began arriving mid-morning and continued to trickle in throughout the day until the house overflowed. Daniel and his cousins played in the barn and waded in the creek and climbed trees. The grown-ups ate indoors. But the children ate outdoors on a table made of sawhorses and boards.

Afterward, those who had a distance to travel said

their good-byes and set off with some daylight left. But Jack's and Anna's families and others who lived nearby gathered in chairs on the summer porch.

The men talked weather and crops; the women, gardens and recipes and fashions in clothing and dress patterns. As shadows began to fall, the conversation shifted to the west, and Indian lore. The spirit world. The happy hunting ground. Old dances forbidden, and the new dance, too. The one Daniel's father had called a "Messiah Dance," or "Ghost Dance."

Daniel saw Jack gape and chew his lip as Pierce repeated what he had told Daniel and Gram and Hattie at dinner the other night about the Messiah coming as an Indian for his Indian children.

"His followers have been told that if they dance and sing the songs he teaches, they'll be lifted up, then lowered again on a restored earth, where the buffalo and wild game will be plentiful again and they can live the old way with their resurrected dead."

"What about us?" Jack spoke up.

"That depends on who you ask," said Pierce. "Some say that non-Indians will be pushed back across the ocean. According to others, we'll be covered over by waves of dirt."

"And they believe this?"

"Some do, some don't. Some are waiting to see." Pierce rubbed a calloused palm against his trouser leg and murmured into the silence, "Things are pretty bleak for the Sioux right now. It makes them vulnerable in a way they never were in their glory years."

Daniel's Story

Daniel saw Jack edging away. Remembering the carved pony and Indian doll, he slipped inside and brought them downstairs for Jack and Anna to see.

Jack scratched a freckle-glazed cheek and ran his fingers over the bent legs of the horse. "Nice," he said with a careless glance. "If we had some sheets, we could play Indian."

"Sheets?" Anna smoothed the Indian doll's braided hair. "Indians don't wear sheets. Do they, Daniel?"

"Sheets, blankets. What's the difference?" said Jack. "Come on with us, Anna. And bring Johnny. I've got an idea."

Daniel followed Jack off the summer porch. He turned back to see Anna poke the Indian doll in her apron pocket and catch their two-year-old cousin Johnny by the hand.

Jack stopped midway across the yard and waited for Anna and Johnny to catch up. "That's a nice blanket you've got there," he said to Johnny.

Johnny stuffed his stubby thumb and one corner of his blanket into his mouth.

Jack squatted beside him. "I'll trade you for it. Looky here at the horse. He's galloping, see?"

"He's getting it sticky," Daniel complained as his little cousin took the horse. "Give it here, Johnny."

Johnny let out an ear-splitting squall. The grown-ups stopped talking and looked their way. Johnny's mother came to her feet. Reluctantly, Daniel gave up trying to retrieve the horse. Johnny toddled back to the house, taking it with him.

"What we have to figure out is how we're going to escape the dirt," said Jack.

"What dirt?" asked Anna.

"The Ghost Dance dirt. The new layer of earth."

"We'll dance. Like this," said Anna. She danced the doll over the grass. "Here he goes, up to the sky." She lifted the doll overhead.

"We need a drum to make it real," said Jack.

They trotted out to the old log cabin toolshed and found an empty nail keg half hidden in the weeds. Daniel ducked inside for a dried gourd Grampa had never gotten around to making into a birdhouse. Jack gave it a shake.

"A drum *and* a shaker," Anna said, beaming.

Daniel turned the keg upside down. He knocked off the dirt and the spiderwebs with a stick.

"Put the doll down and dance, Anna," said Jack. He tossed her Johnny's blanket. "Wrap it around you. That's the way."

Anna stood on tiptoe and put the doll in the low fork of a nearby pear tree. "Pretend the branches are clouds. Beat the drum, Daniel."

Daniel whacked the nail keg with his stick. Jack shook the rattling gourd. Anna waved her arms and shuffled in place. Damp curls clung to her forehead. Dusk fell. Fireflies rose from the grass.

"Hey, I know!" said Jack. He gave the gourd to Daniel and scrambled up the tree and out on a branch. "Hold up your arms, Anna. Where I can reach 'em."

Anna groped the air with her fingers as she danced.

Jack hung by his knees from the branch and tried to catch her hands.

"Hurry! The waves are coming!" squealed Anna.

"You have to sing," reminded Jack.

"'Ashes to ashes, dust to dust,'" sang Daniel.

"Lift me, lift me!"

"I'm trying." Jack clasped Anna's wrists. He huffed and puffed and tugged.

"Nine, eight, seven, six," Daniel counted down. "Five, four, three, two—hold your breath, Anna. Here comes the dirt!"

Jack's cheeks pouched like ripe apples. With a mighty heave, he jerked Anna off the ground.

"I'm rising. I beat the dirt!" Anna cried, dangling inches from the ground. "Yikes. Johnny's giving the horse a drink."

Daniel spun around to see Johnny in the flowers, dipping his horse into Gram's watering can. He dropped his stick and gourd, jerked the blanket from Anna's shoulders, and raced across the yard.

His father saw Johnny, too. And the horse. His mouth flattened as he darted to the rescue.

Chapter Fourteen

Pierce reached Johnny a step ahead of Daniel.

"You rode him hard, didn't you, cowboy?" he said, taking the horse from the watering can. "And gave him a nice drink. Looks to me like he's ready for the stables."

His voice was mild, his expression, too. But he was careful with the wooden horse, shaking the water off, rubbing it dry. Daniel fidgeted, wishing he could explain that it was Jack who had given Johnny the horse.

Instead, he gave Johnny his blanket and returned to the pear tree.

Jack and Anna had abandoned their Ghost Dance. They were swinging through the gate at the edge of the yard. "Come on!" called Anna. "Jack's got a better idea."

"In a minute," said Daniel. He retrieved the buckskin doll from the fork of the tree where Anna had left it and took it to the house.

Anna's older sisters and the boardinghouse cook were washing dishes in the kitchen. Daniel climbed up onto a chair and put the Indian doll on a high shelf, where there was no risk of it falling into careless hands. He caught up with Jack and Anna on the path to the boardinghouse.

"Sheets! See?" Anna said, pointing to the clothesline

strung across the backyard. "We're going to be ghosts!"

As they reached the backyard, Daniel saw that it wasn't sheets. It was dish towels and shirts hanging from the line.

"Close enough," said Jack. "Wait'll it's dark, and we'll jump at the first feller out the door."

"*Boo!*" Anna threw her hands wide and giggled in anticipation.

Daniel hunkered down at the edge of the herb garden beside Jack and peeked through a border of knee-high sage. Anna wiggled in between them. The pungent scent stirred a vague and disagreeable association. Daniel's nose twitched. "Chaldea!" he blurted out, sitting up. "She was supposed to cook supper for the men tonight."

"She's gone by now, late as it is," reasoned Jack.

Trees twittered. Branches scratched the shingled roof built over the backyard well. *Like bony fingers.* "If you see her, run," Daniel whispered to Anna.

"What for?" asked Anna.

"She's a witch."

"She is not. Is she, Jack?" said Anna.

"Sure she is," said Jack. "She reads the future from the stars. Honest! Earl's seen her. She prowls the cemeteries, too, and mumbles to the dead."

"Huh-uh," said Anna.

Jack's eyes shone like twin moons. "Tell you something else, too—Earl's heard 'em answer."

"Huh-uh!"

"Uh-huh!"

"What'd they say, then?" asked Anna.

"They talk different from us. It's a dead language—sounds like wind moaning through trees." Jack imitated a low, moany voice.

"Huh-uh," said Anna. But she edged closer to Daniel.

Soon, the only light to be seen glowed from the kitchen window. Jack streaked to the clothesline. Pitched the prop to one side. Jerked at towels and shirts off the drooping clothesline and darted back.

The shirts were clean. But the towels were damp. Daniel covered his head and wrinkled his nose. "I can't see."

"You got your knife? Give it here, and I'll cut eyeholes," offered Jack.

Daniel cut the holes himself. He cut eyeholes for Jack and Anna, too. Jack broke straws to see who would slip up and rattle the window so someone would come out.

But before they could draw, two men strolled out on the porch and down the steps. They ambled to the laundry bench at the corner of the house and sat with their backs to the children.

"Now!" whispered Jack.

He stole across the yard and evaporated into shadows, with Anna at his heels. Daniel sailed over the damp grass, goose bumped and goggle-eyed, trying to make out shapes in the dark. Past the well. Under the clothesline.

There was an old skillet near the back steps. Daniel

didn't see it until it stuck out its handle and tripped him. His shins yelped. His dish towel sailed past the toppled skillet. The back door opened. He swiveled on hands and knees and willy-nilly nerves as lamplight thrust a dark shape forward. *Chaldea!* The screen door slammed her name.

Three thumping strides and she loomed over the steps. Her hexing hands went up. Cats leaped from all directions. Matter hurled through the air and sloshed over Daniel. It slid down his face and oozed off his chin.

He shot up, spun around howling, and plowed into the clothesline, trying to escape Chaldea's hex. The rope line throttled his shriek and knocked him sky-goggle. His feet flew one way, his head the other.

Stars exploded, diamond bright, and winked out like spent fireworks. Muted feet and Anna's screams. Whisper soft. Fading, fading as a wave of dark earth covered him over.

Chapter Fifteen

A hum, fly-pesky, pierced the darkness. Trilling, rumbling right against his ear. Sandy, wet, and warm. Daniel cracked one eyelid and clutched his throbbing throat. A purring tabby licked his cheek.

He pushed it away and saw faces peering down at him. Two were bearded, the third a stone in a firebrand setting.

Chaldea! Leaping cats and witches' brew! Daniel tore grass retreating on fingernails, elbows, and heels.

"Easy, son. You're head's bleeding," warned one of the men.

"Yarrow will clot it," said Chaldea. She set off for the house.

Daniel tried to protest. But his throat was all knots and scattered needles. The men hoisted him to his feet. The dewy, dark yard swam before his eyes.

"There, there," sympathized one as they eased him down on the laundry bench.

"Miss Jennings will fix you right up," chimed the other.

Chaldea's silhouette crossed the lamp-lit kitchen window. *Getting her weedy remedies ready.*

God? It's Daniel, here.

"Daniel?"

Daniel's heart bucked. But it was his flesh-and-blood father striding across the yard, calling his name.

"Over here," one of the workmen called back. "He hit his head on the well."

"You're wet," Pierce said, dropping beside him. "What've you got all over you?"

"Witches' brew," Daniel rasped, his hands lapped over his throat.

"What's that?" his father said, cupping his ear.

"Bricks knocked him out cold. He's collecting his wits."

The other hired hand turned as Chaldea stepped out on the porch. "Leave him to Miss Jennings. She'll clean him up."

Daniel cowered against his father. "Hattie will . . . tell her," he forced words past his burning throat.

"We don't want to put you out, ma'am," said Pierce, after checking the rope burn on Daniel's neck. "I'll take him on home, thanks all the same. Whose shirt?"

"Mine, if it came off the line," one of the men spoke up.

"Did it?" asked Pierce.

Daniel nodded and stripped out of it.

"Worse for the wear," said his father. "I'm sorry, sir. I don't know what he's got into."

"It's leftovers. I threw table scraps to the cats," Chaldea said, words stiff as her skirts were wilty. "It was dark, I didn't see him."

Daniel itched and twitched and edged away, leaving

Chaldea to her side of the story. His father wasn't long in catching up with him. He had the soiled shirt in hand.

"See that it gets washed, starched, pressed, and returned. And next time you go horsing around?" Pierce added. "Save your neck, and prop the clothesline up out of harm's way where you won't hang yourself on it."

Jack and Anna were on the summer porch with the grown-ups. Everyone crowded into the kitchen, all talking at once. Jack winced at the knot on Daniel's head and whistled at the clothesline streak. "Witch wounds!" he exclaimed.

"Now there you go again," said Hattie. "What have I told you about that?" She questioned, patched, and scolded all at the same time.

The gathering soon broke up. Tandys dispersed to their separate homes. Hattie sent Daniel upstairs with a pitcher of hot water and orders to bathe before crawling between clean sheets.

When he had done so, she came upstairs, bid him good night, and whisked his soiled clothing away.

Sometime later, Pierce came to Daniel's room with a cup in his hand. "Warm cocoa," he said. "Hattie sent it."

"She went home?"

"Just now," said Pierce. "We had a long talk. She told me about you and Jack scaring Miss Jennings at the crossing. That you thought she put a spell on you."

"Grampa, too." Daniel's fingernail traced a chip on the lip of the cup. "The train hit Grampa right where she fell off her bicycle."

Daniel's Story

"It was the logical place to cross," his father pointed out.

"He was all right, though, until that day when Jack blew the whistle."

"You're not responsible for his death, if that's what you're thinking," said Pierce. He scraped the floor, pulling up a chair to Daniel's bedside. "No one could anticipate he would go that way. But we did know he wasn't long for this world. He wasn't well, and hadn't been for a while."

"He was getting better, though," said Daniel.

"I'm afraid not," said his father. "Harmony wrote me over a year ago, saying the doctor didn't give him much time."

Daniel gripped the warm cup, his father's words vibrating in his ears.

"They didn't tell you?"

Daniel moved his head from side to side.

"I guess they thought they'd spare you the worry."

But they *had* told his father. Over a thousand miles away. "You knew and you didn't come home?" Daniel said finally.

"I came as soon as I could," said his father. "I have people counting on me."

More important than Grampa? Daniel put his milk aside, untouched. He pulled the sheet up. Burrowed his head beneath his pillow. It straddled his shoulders like a yoke. Only it was Pierce who was yoked. And not to his family.

"Aren't you going to drink your milk?" his father asked.

"My stomach hurts," said Daniel.

If his father replied, he didn't hear him. The pillow muffled sounds. When Daniel peeked from beneath it, the cup was gone, and his father, too.

Chapter Sixteen

The next morning, Gram complained she had not slept, and said her good-byes at the house. Daniel went to the crossing to see his father off. His father's younger brothers and some cousins gathered there, too. The women hugged Pierce. The men shook hands. They were strongly built farmers, and well weathered. Yet Pierce stood out from the rest in his buckskin coat, fringed gloves, and black boots that reached his knees.

Daniel sucked his cheek, trying to coax the comparison to light in bold strokes and gray shadows. A whistle whined in the distance, rushing his efforts. He penciled in the tracks snaking out of heavy timber.

The ground trembled. The trees quaked. Cattle bellowed from holding pens. The train crawled out of the trees and shuddered to a stop, closing off the rural crossing. A man scrambled up on the tinder. He pulled the rope on the water tank spout and gave the train a drink.

Daniel's hand raced to the finish as Pierce's shadow fell over the page.

"Ready?" he said.

Daniel scrawled his name and turned up the sketch. "Me?"

Daniel nodded. "There's more. You want to see?"

"I wish there were time," said Pierce.

Nearby, the engine pipped like a clock, eating up moments. Daniel struggled with himself, then thrust the tablet at his father. "Take it with you."

"Are you sure?" said Pierce.

Daniel nodded.

Pierce tucked the tablet beneath one arm. "I'd send you something in exchange if I thought the mail would go through."

"It will," said Daniel. "It always does."

"Does it?"

Pierce reached in his pocket. The seal was broken on the letter he withdrew. It was the undelivered note for Mr. Nelson. Daniel swallowed, his head achy and his throat still sore from last night.

"I knocked the saddlebag off the wall, putting your horse away," his father continued. "I meant to ask you about it last night. But it slipped my mind, what with all the excitement."

Daniel dug his toe in the dirt, and didn't look up.

"Seems odd you'd write twice asking for a note, then not pass it along when I sent it," Pierce prompted. "You want to clear that up for me?"

"I didn't want to get Jack in trouble," Daniel said when silence failed to spare him.

"You read it, then?" said his father.

Daniel's ears burned. "Yes, sir."

"Strikes me Jack's a little reckless. With himself and with others, too."

"He doesn't mean to be," said Daniel.

"I know that. Believe me, I know." His father appeared to have more to say. But the conductor gave the boarding call. He hardened his jaw and drew himself up, tall and straight. "When's school start?"

"September ninth."

"You give it to your teacher first day back. Or I can mail it direct, take your choice."

Daniel took the letter.

"Give him my address while you're at it," said Pierce. "You hear me?"

"Yes, sir."

His father picked up his grip. "Come on, then, and see me off."

The grip, a black leather contraption, slapped between them as they walked to the train. Daniel offered his hand. His father reached past it, and hugged him close. "I'm going to miss you, Scout."

"I could go with you," Daniel offered, eyes stinging.

"You could. But not just yet."

Daniel stepped out of his father's embrace. He coughed and cleared his lungs of mingled leather and Prince Albert Tobacco.

"Harmony's going to be lost without Father," said Pierce. "You look after her, and don't give her any worry."

Daniel's gut churned with a rush of sorrow that was Gram's grief and the loss of Grampa and of his father all wrapped together.

Pierce boarded the train. A moment later, his face appeared at the coach window. Couplings clanged as the car rolled forward. He had arrived in sunshine and left in the same. It glittered like fool's gold, glazing the trees and misting Daniel's eyes.

A familiar arm settled across his shoulder. "There, there," murmured Hattie. "He'll be back."

Would he? Then why did his leave-taking seem just as final as Grampa's?

Chapter Seventeen

In coming days, Gram's treadle machine hummed and shimmied and shook at all hours. She kept busy stitching drab-colored scrap pieces into what Hattie said was to be a variation of a Jacob's Ladder quilt. "Underground Railroad," Hattie called it.

"She's working out her grief," Hattie explained.

Grampa's empty place at the table, his chair by the stove, and the silence his voice used to fill gave Daniel pangs, too. But a person couldn't be sad all the time. He couldn't, anyway. Not when the sky poured sunshine and days dawned like a fresh sheet of paper waiting for pencil lead.

Most mornings, he left the house right after breakfast and trotted over to Earl's syrup camp. Earl had big plans for next season. He was putting up a building for the evaporator he had ordered from a factory in Vermont. It would boil sap more efficiently and with less trouble than iron kettles. Daniel went to the crossing with him and Jack the day it came in.

It took several men to help Earl load the crate into the wagon. When they got it to the camp, Earl pried the lid off. "See there? The pans are channeled," he said. "The sap goes in raw at one end. It moves through the pans as it cooks, and as you draw it off, syrup."

"Nice," said Jack. "Can we have the box?"

The crate was spacious, deep and wide, and several feet longer than Daniel was tall.

"What'll we do with it?" Daniel asked once the men had unloaded the evaporator.

"Make a sod box," said Jack.

Daniel slapped a mosquito off his chin and waited for Jack to explain.

"For the Ghost Dance," Jack obliged him. "We'll put dirt in it, see. And whoever doesn't dance gets dirty."

"How?" asked Daniel.

Jack thunked the crate, testing the wood. It was solidly built, with no holes for sprinkling out dirt. "Drill holes in the bottom. Then we can fill it with dirt and—"

"How you going to keep dirt in it with holes in the bottom?"

Jack cocked his hands on his hips and jutted out his freckled chin. "You got a better idea?"

Daniel circled the box, thinking it over. He climbed inside, lay down, and stretched his arms wide.

"Well?" prompted Jack.

"How about we make a trapdoor on one side of the box? We can pop it open, tilt the box, and spill the dirt out."

What with Earl's demands on their time, and other setbacks, it took several days to complete the trapdoor. It finished out at about two-feet square, with hinges made from leather strips.

Jack and Daniel levered the lid to the crate in the fork of a tree where the main limbs branched off in four directions. The crate was a good deal heavier. Getting it up the tree was no easy feat. After several failed attempts, they attached the ropes to Boots and used horsepower to hoist it up.

The same arrangement worked well for filling the box with dirt. Jack climbed the tree, looped a rope over a branch, and tossed it back down to Daniel. He rigged that end to Boots, and the other to the bucket of dirt. As Boots moved forward, the bucket was lifted into the tree, where Jack emptied it into the crate. Daniel guided Boots into retreat, thereby lowering the bucket to the ground again.

It was a good system. For Jack, anyway. Daniel did all the digging. The soil was dark and loose. But dodging tree roots made uphill work of it. "Isn't it about enough?" he called to Jack, up in the tree.

"Not nearly," said Jack. "Box isn't even half full."

"You dig, then." Daniel put the shovel to one side and rested his blisters.

Jack dug until half was enough. They were arguing over who was going to dump from above and who was going to dance below, when some grown-up cousins came along to help Earl set the rafters on his sap-cooking house. Matthew was with them. Anna had tagged along, too.

"Hey, Anna! You wanna play Ghost Dance?" Jack hollered from the tree.

Anna joined Daniel beneath the tree. Her pigtails

dangled like ravelings as she gaped into the branches. "Where's Jack?"

"Right here." A hand waved from a screen of leaves. "Here comes a rope. Hold on to it, and I'll pull you up when the dirt waves come."

Jack didn't warn her it would be real dirt.

Daniel caught the free end of the rope and held it out of Anna's reach. "Wait a second," he said to Jack. "You can't—"

"I can, too!" Anna said, misunderstanding. "I *can* climb a rope! Watch me."

"Yeah, but—"

"What's a little dirt on the noggin? Give her the rope," ordered Jack. "I'll be the drummer. You can knock some sticks together."

Anna wrinkled her face at Daniel and grabbed the rope. Daniel crowded out his misgivings and shrugged. "All right, then. Just remember whose idea it was."

Jack pounded the crate with a hammer. "I can't hear you, Daniel!"

Daniel found two stout sticks well clear of the tree, and beat them together.

Anna grabbed the rope and danced a Maypole Dance. "Sing with me, Daniel!"

"You're awful bossy," he complained.

"Here we go round the Maypole, the Maypole. Hey! The maple." Anna stopped singing and giggled. "Did you hear that? Here we go round the Maypole . . ."

"Anna, Anna, in her ghost shirt. Here comes the dirt," Daniel chanted over her singing.

He looked up. Waited. Nothing happened.

"Anna, Anna on the piana," he tried again. "Here comes the dirt."

Still nothing.

"Anna, Anna, climb the rope. It's your only hope."

Anna climbed several feet in the air. "See! I told you!" she hollered, and poked her tongue out at Daniel.

Daniel narrowed his eyes and cupped his mouth with his hands. "Jack, Jack. Don't hold back. Where's the dirt?" he yelled.

"Hey! Jack!" Earl strode beneath the tree. "I've been looking all over for that hammer. Toss it down here."

Jack tossed, but it wasn't a hammer. Anna shrieked and lost her grip and fell on Earl in a hail of dirt. He leaped up, shaking off Anna and rich, black timber soil the way a dog shakes off rainwater.

Jack dangled from the overhead branch, all red-faced freckles and laughter. Earl set Anna on her feet and skinned up the rope. The tree was a fury of rustling branches, Jack-hoots, and Earl-threats. But for all Earl's heat, he came down empty-handed. Except for his hammer.

"He got dirt in my hair!" complained Anna.

"Mine, too," said Earl. "But he has to come down sometime. And then we'll fix him."

"Yeah. We'll fix him," Anna echoed with a pert nod.

Earl tugged her braid and strode off, swinging his hammer and whistling.

Daniel wondered how long it would take Jack to sneak down out of the tree. Longer than he wanted to wait, probably. His belly was chiming like a noonday clock. All in all, it had been a full morning. Their efforts had paid off. The trapdoor was a dirt-raining success. And for once, it was Jack caught out on a limb.

"Where you going?" Anna asked as Daniel turned for home.

"Home for lunch."

"Can I come?"

"Ask your dad," said Daniel.

Chapter Eighteen

Anna asked. But Matthew said no, that Hattie had more than she could do just to look after Gram. Daniel thought that was an excuse until he arrived home and found Chaldea at the stove.

She turned and saw him before he could retreat out the door. "Lunch is ready," she said.

"Where's Hattie?" he asked.

"In the sitting room." Chaldea poured lunch into a soup tureen on the table and turned to the sink with the empty pan.

Daniel caught a glimpse of shaved beef and noodles pale as death. And something green. It smelled like sage. He crowded the far wall and sidled off to the parlor. Gram was at one end of the Moorish divan, Hattie at the other. A quilt top spanned their laps.

"So there you are," Hattie said, looking up from her needlework. "We were just wondering about you. Maralee's waiting dinner."

"What's *she* doing here?" asked Daniel.

"Filling in for me while Aunt Harmony and I stitch this quilt top together," said Hattie. She reached over and patted Gram's hand. "We could have it ready for the frame by tomorrow. Shall I send for the girls, Aunt Harmony? Or do you think the weekend would be better for them?"

"I believe I'll quilt it myself, Hattie."

"Oh, but a quilting bee would be fun," cajoled Hattie.

"If you can tolerate the commotion," Gram said, her scarred cheeks taut as railway switches. "I can't. Not yet, anyway."

Daniel gave the quilt top a second look. It was dark and broody. "Who's it for?" he asked.

"Have you decided yet, Aunt Harmony?" asked Hattie.

Gram scratched her temple with her thimbled finger, shrugged, and went on stitching.

Hattie patted Gram again and came to her feet. She ushered Daniel out of the parlor and closed the door. "I want to talk to you about Maralee. She's going to be helping out around here."

"Why? Are you going somewhere?" Daniel asked, alarmed.

Hattie's gaze slid away. "I don't like Aunt Harmony spending so much time alone. She won't go out and she won't invite anyone in, and I can't be everywhere at once."

"But why Chaldea?" asked Daniel.

"*Maralee* needs the work," Hattie said, her tone heavy with emphasis. "She doesn't meddle. And Aunt Harmony is comfortable with her."

"I'm not."

Hattie sighed. "Just be polite. Now go wash up, and we'll eat."

Daniel's Story

"I'm not hungry," said Daniel.

It was hot upstairs. Daniel flung himself on the bed, locked his hands behind his head, and scowled at the ceiling. His belly grumbled. He muttered and mumbled and held his breath, listening.

But Hattie didn't call his name. She didn't come looking to say she'd thought it over and decided they could make other arrangements for house help.

Swimming in his own sweat, Daniel hauled himself down the back stairs. Hushed voices reached him. He stopped a couple of steps from the bottom and listened.

"If you don't want to, don't," Chaldea's voice rustled like weeds.

"How can I not? Our place is with him," replied Hattie.

"What about the boy? Have you told him you're going?"

Daniel's stomach dropped like dirt from the sod box. "Going where?" he wailed from the stairs.

Oklahoma Territory, come September. Matthew was set on it, Hattie said. She got tears in her eyes, and Daniel, for all his hurt, couldn't plead his own case.

He bottled it up and his own made-up mind, too. Climbed the stairs and emptied his saddlebag treasury. Jack came along as he was counting his savings. He was wet and smelled of the creek.

"It got hot in that tree. I went for a swim." Jack plucked a twig from his hair and grinned, admitting, "With a little help from Earl."

"Did you see her in the kitchen?" asked Daniel.

"Chaldea?" Jack nodded. "Is she making Aunt Harmony a tonic?"

"No, she's taking Hattie's place."

"You don't mean it! Then Hattie's going?"

"To Oklahoma Territory," Daniel said, heat rising behind his eyes.

"I'd have bet anything Matthew couldn't talk her into it." Jack's soppy shoes squeaked as he crossed the room. He hit the window facing with the flat of his hand and whistled low. "I wouldn't want Chaldea working at my house."

"You think I do?"

"So what're you going to do?"

"Go live with my dad."

Jack retraced his steps, lips pursed, a wrinkle in his chin. "When are you leaving?"

"Soon as I can."

"Hattie's pulling up roots right away?"

"Not until September."

"Then what's your rush?" asked Jack.

"Chaldea! She cooked today."

"Oh, boy," said Jack. "You'd better go, then. Don't worry. I'll help you."

They went out to the woods where there was no danger of being overheard. Daniel discarded the idea of buying the ticket locally for fear word would get back to Gram.

Jack offered to buy the ticket for him the next time he went to Bloomington. No one would know him there.

Daniel's Story

Or make the connection when Daniel disappeared.

Daniel prayed over coming days that Hattie would change her mind. Or that if he didn't eat Chaldea's cooking, Gram would see him getting skinny and fire her. Neither happened. He tried to talk to Gram about it. But she was living in a patchwork world. If she had an opinion on Hattie being uprooted or Chaldea filling the root hole, she was keeping it to herself.

It was the last week in August when Jack went to Bloomington with his mother to buy school clothes. They stayed overnight with relatives. But to Daniel's disappointment, the agent at the station refused to sell Jack the ticket.

"How come?"

"Said I was too young, and to send my mother or father in," replied Jack. "Don't worry, though. I've thought about it all the way home and I've got it all figured out."

Daniel lifted his chin off the floor.

"Remember that runaway slave Mr. Nelson told us about last year? The one they mailed to freedom?" Jack went on.

Disappointed, Daniel sighed. "Not that again."

"That's right!" Jack's freckled cheeks gleamed like brown sugar on apple dumplings. "I'm going to ship you there in the sod box."

Daniel thought all day and all night, trying to come up with a better solution. Failing at that, he took it up with Jack again the next day. "Five days is a long time to be in a box," he began.

"It isn't like you'll be staying in the crate," argued Jack. "You'll be in a baggage car, more'n likely. Won't be anyone about. Except when you change trains."

"I have to change trains?"

"Five or six times. But don't worry—you're freight. That's the beauty of it, don't you see?" said Jack. His eyes shone the way they always did when he got inspired by an idea. "You'll get there without even having to think or talk or anything. You can slip out the trapdoor whenever you want to stretch your legs. And we'll make it real comfortable for sleeping."

"I guess I could take covers," said Daniel.

"And food," said Jack.

"Water."

"And a pee can. Just in case you need it. Why, it'll be almost as good as having your own private railway car."

"What if I get caught?"

"You're not doing anything wrong, as long as you've paid the freight," reasoned Jack.

"How, if I'm in the box?" asked Daniel.

"I'm working on that one."

"Work fast," said Daniel. "Hattie's leaving in a week."

Chapter Nineteen

As it turned out, Daniel himself came up with a plan. His uncles helped, though not on purpose. They wanted to push in the old log cabin toolshed. But they had to clean it out first and sort through what was worth keeping. Gram told them to divide the contents among themselves. Pierce, they agreed, should get a share, too.

Daniel and Jack dragged the sod box home from the syrup camp. They had it ready and waiting when Daniel's uncles came on Saturday. Daniel helped the men empty the cabin out. Any useful items they didn't want, they put in the crate for his father.

One of Daniel's uncles nailed the crate shut just before dusk. Daniel followed him to the boarding-house. He listened as his uncle made arrangements with one of the hired men to haul the crate to the crossing on Monday. He gave the man money to pay the shipping.

Jack showed up after dark as prearranged. They dragged the crate out to the barn, unloaded it by lantern light, and hid the contents in the loft.

The next day, after church, Daniel repacked the crate with what he would need for his trip. Chaldea didn't work on Sundays. Hattie was at home, packing to go to Oklahoma. Gram was taking a nap. There was no rush, and little risk of discovery.

Daniel took jerked beef from the smokehouse. He packed fresh apples, freshly dug potatoes, and home-canned peaches and cherries Hattie had preserved in blue mason jars. He wired the jars in place so they wouldn't shift about and painted on the top of the crate: BREAKABLE. THIS SIDE UP.

From the kitchen, he snitched bread and the last half of the pie Hattie had baked on Friday. He filled two canteens with water. He wrapped bread, fruit, and potatoes snugly inside the Pony Express saddlebag, along with his sketchbook, pencils, and his savings. He padded the crate with a couple of old quilts and his winter coat.

Jack came late in the afternoon. He prowled through the crate, double-checking Daniel's supplies. Jack talked him into sharing the apple pie in place of saying good-bye. Then Jack climbed up on his pony and stretched out a hand to Daniel.

Daniel shuffled his feet. "I thought we just said good-bye."

"We did," Jack said, a small jeweler's box in his palm. "It's a present. Take off the lid."

Daniel removed the lid and jumped back. Inside, a severed finger lay on a wad of cotton. It *looked* like a severed finger, anyway. Until it wiggled.

"Got you!" Jack slapped his knee and laughed.

Daniel grinned and turned the box over. There was

a hole in the bottom, hidden by the cotton. He stuck his finger through the hole, held it snug against the cotton wadding and put the lid on. "Five days, Jack," he said. "Then you tell them where I am."

"Not a day sooner. I promise," said Jack.

Gram quilted after supper. Daniel joined her in the parlor, but couldn't sit still. He paced, running his hand along the Moorish divan, plucking at the snags in the Chinese screen, sticking his nose in some flowers Hattie had arranged in a vase.

"Bedtime," Gram said, after a while.

Daniel hugged her neck, then kissed her scarred cheek.

"My, my," she murmured with a faint smile. "What have you been into now?"

"Nothing," said Daniel. He turned for the steps and, halfway up, called back, "Night, Gram. I love you."

Once in bed, Daniel's thoughts churned with Gram and Jack and Earl and the syrup camp and school, soon to begin. Hattie and Anna and Matthew and the girls crept into the mix. He wished he could see them one last time.

The downstairs clock in the formal parlor tolled midnight. Then one, then two. By three o'clock Daniel was so tired, he was afraid if he went to sleep, he wouldn't wake up in time to get in the crate before the hired man came.

At four, he slipped outside with his pillow, crawled into the crate, and secured the trapdoor from the inside.

*

It was a dream that stirred Daniel's rest. A dream of Hattie. She shook the whole kitchen with her pacing.

"I could whip Jack for doing this to you, and you for letting him!" she exclaimed. "It's lazy not to do your own thinking."

Then it was Chaldea, pacing, dragging him along by the ear. She wasn't talking at all. But she had cat claws for fingernails.

Daniel winced and rubbed his ear. A nail was poking him. Not a fingernail. A *crate* nail. The rocking wasn't Hattie's storming feet shaking the floor. It wasn't a lumbering wagon, either. It had too much sound and fury to it, too much sway and too much power. And the smell of burning coal.

Daniel heard a whistle scream and a bell clang. He had slept right through the ride to the crossing, and the loading, too! He banged his head on the crate. It was dark. Too dark for telling time or sketching or anything else. Unless he got out and found some daylight.

Daniel slid his hand along one side of the crate, looking for the trapdoor latch. The door gave a little, but refused to fall open. He pushed harder. But his crate was firmly wedged. His heart sank. He was stuck inside the crate!

The walls of the box closed in on Daniel. He cupped his hands to his face and breathed the air he had trapped. It was like being behind the map when he missed a question playing Mr. Nelson's geography game. Only worse. Behind the map, he could have called to

Mr. Nelson for permission to return to his seat. Now, if he called out for help, he would be found out and maybe put off the train.

Daniel squeezed his eyes shut tight and fought the cornered feeling with his mind. He probed the walls of the crate. They weren't really folding in, threatening to crush him. And it wasn't shortage of air stabbing his lungs. There were holes in the crate. He proved it to himself by breathing deeply. Five. Ten, twenty times with no sign of running out of air.

Daniel retrieved Grampa's folded knife from his pocket. He didn't open it. The worn ivory handle warmed against his palm. Anna's made-up song fit itself to the rhythmic clickety-clack of iron wheels over rails:

> Here we go round the Maypole,
> the Maypole.
> the Maypole.

Slowly, the tight ache in his lungs receded. His pulse returned to normal. His heartbeat, too. Hoping Jack was right about changing trains, Daniel prayed the first switch would come soon.

Chapter Twenty

Daniel thought he had gone a good distance when the train began to slow. He braced himself so as not to roll when the crate was unloaded onto a high-wheeled baggage cart. He put his eye to a knothole in the crate and saw that it was the Bloomington station. He was only fifteen miles from home. But at least when the baggage car door slammed shut, his crate was positioned where he could crawl out once it seemed safe to do so. In the meantime, he needed to answer nature's call.

It was cramped quarters, but Daniel got the job done, then turned his attention to his growling belly. He was eating beef jerky and bread when he felt the train begin to slow. His crate changed trains, this time in Peoria. He had been to Peoria once with Grampa to hear a Fourth of July speaker. The speaker was dull, but the fireworks were wonderful.

There was an abrupt and not-so-wonderful reenactment of them when a baggage man, using a handcart to wheel him into the bowels of the baggage car, let his crate fall. One moment, Daniel was upright like a mummy in a coffin. The next he was flat on his face, hearing bombs blast.

"Oops," muttered the baggage man.

The bombs were Daniel's food stash. In an upside-down position, the blue mason jars had slipped free of their wires and crashed together, breaking as they fell. Daniel felt a syrupy gumbo of preserved fruit spreading about his shins and seeping through his trousers. Fearful of cutting himself on broken glass, he gripped the bottom of the crate with his knees and lifted his lower legs out of the muck as best he could.

"Numskulls," mumbled the baggage man. "Ort ta know better'n ship glass without packin's. Ain't up to John Jeffrey ta mollycoddle 'em along."

Daniel's crate, to the accompaniment of broken glass, tumbling vegetables, and flying personal effects, was levered once more into an upright position. Pivoted half a turn. Rolled deeper into the baggage car. And dropped once more.

"Nincompoops," the baggage man pronounced a final eulogy as he laid Daniel to rest. Faceup this time and, miraculously, unhurt.

Somehow, Daniel escaped being cut by the broken mason jars. But his supplies were a casualty of John Jeffrey's carelessness. So was the pee can. He had had no chance to empty it. It was empty now. His crate was a mess, and so was he.

John Jeffrey had done only one good turn: He had not left Daniel's crate wedged in. Once they were underway again, Daniel opened the trapdoor. He listened intently and at length to be sure he was alone. Finally, he crawled out.

There were windowed doors at both ends of the near-empty baggage car. It wasn't much light. But it was enough. Daniel passed the miles cleaning up the mess. He used a broken jar as a container and a galvanized jar lid as a shovel. The door at the nearest end of the car opened at his touch. He emptied the jar from the narrow platform between cars and repeated the process until his crate was habitable again.

Water from one canteen was insufficient for cleaning his clothes. But it did stretch far enough to clean his hands and face. Uncertain when he would get the chance to replenish his supply, he saved the second canteen for drinking.

His food supply, once so plentiful, was now a concern. He had salvaged only his apples and potatoes. Raw potatoes didn't sound too tempting. But when it got dark, he peeled and ate one, and an apple, too. His quilts were damp and sticky. So was his coat and pillow. Despite his discomfort, the swaying rocked him to sleep.

And so passed his first day.

The second day crept by in similar fashion. By the third, Daniel was out of food. He had changed trains again. The car he was riding in was a combination baggage and coach with a door between. There was a small pane of glass in the door. On tiptoe, he could see into the passenger section. Gaslights hung from the clerestory roof. The roof was lower over the seats where the passengers sat at their ease. Some watched the country pass by the train windows. Others read or ate lunches they had brought along.

At the front of the car, Daniel could see a stove and,

beyond that, a side door through which people came and went. After a while he realized it was a lavatory. There were empty seats. The comforts of coach travel beckoned invitingly. Yet a glimpse of the conductor in his pillbox hat and double-breasted suit with its big, shiny buttons was enough to discourage Daniel from acting upon the temptation. "I'm freight," he reminded himself aloud.

Freight had to be careful about peeking in on folks, or sneaking out on the open platform at the rear of the baggage section and getting dizzy watching as the tracks flew by below.

Once, as Daniel stood on the open-air platform in the deafening rattle of wheels grating rails, he saw a man riding the rods. The train was moving along at thirty miles an hour or better. But there the fellow stood, clinging to the wooden sides of the swaying car, his feet on the support rods, the wind in his whiskers and the sun burning his bald head. "Howdy!" he hollered. "Where you headed?"

Daniel blinked, then lifted his hand. "South Dakota," he said, and backed inside again.

Daniel didn't leave his crate for the rest of the day. Each exit was a risk. A baggage man, the conductor, or even a passenger could wander through without warning.

The stops were even riskier. Daniel didn't know where he was, or when his crate might be moved to another train. He left the train while it was stopped only once, and that was to fill his canteens and try to buy food.

He was 50-percent successful: He found water.

There was a delay on the fourth day. Daniel didn't know why. All he knew was the only thing moving was his belly. It was rumbling and rolling and growling like a hungry bear.

By the fifth day, his head hurt and he was sleepy. His crate changed trains in the night. Once they were underway, he tried the trapdoor and found he was wedged in again.

He drank some water and made a fifth notch in the crate with his knife and prayed to wake up and find his father popping open the lid.

Chapter Twenty-one

It was the lack of motion that woke Daniel. No rocking or whistling or ringing of a bell. No chuffing or pinging of an engine popping off steam. He rolled to one side in the crate. It reeked of his unwashed body and the pee can. He needed to empty it, and himself, too.

Daniel unlatched the trapdoor and saw by outdoor night lamps that he had been unloaded onto a railway platform beside a station marked Valentine, Nebraska. Valentine! His father worked out of Valentine. The town was just a hair south of the South Dakota line. His father could be right here, right now, picking up freight to deliver. Or soon to, anyway. Once day broke.

A starless breeze bathed Daniel's goose bumps as he crawled out of his crate. Concealed by clustered trunks, boxes, and baggage, he took a careful look around. Seeing no one, he retrieved his can and closed the trapdoor.

Daniel moved away from the platform and into the shadows of goods piled along the siding. He braced himself between sacks of flour and bales of blankets, wiggling numb limbs, waiting for his strength to return. The aroma of coffee beans and plug tobacco mingled with the cidery scent of apples in nail-tight crates. There was sugar, too. And wooden boxes of foodstuffs, the likes of which would have filled Mr. Walker's shelves a dozen times over.

"What're you doin' there, boy?"

Daniel backed away as a soldier stepped into his path. "Looking for something to eat," his empty stomach put words on his lips.

"This is United States government provisions. You don't want to be helping yourself," the soldier said, shifting his rifle.

Daniel twitched and pulled his gaze away from the apple crates.

"Hungry?"

Daniel nodded.

The soldier shifted his weight, squinting at him in the gray before dawn. "The hotel'll be throwing out their breakfast leavin's by and by, if you don't mind scavengering with the Indians."

"Scavengering?" Daniel echoed, uncertain of the word.

"Runaways got to eat, same as Sioux and soldiers."

"I didn't run away," said Daniel. "I'm looking for my father."

The soldier laid his finger aside his nose and looked about. "You don't see him anywheres, do you? Now scat, before somebody comes along and mistakes you for trouble."

Daniel plodded out of reach of burning lamps and signalmen and soldiers. He took care of business, then kicked the can away. What did he need with it now? What he *did* need was the name of the freighting company that employed his father. The horizon flushed pink as he tried to pick it out of his memory.

Patches of bristly grass rustled underfoot. Sleepy birds chirped. But the name wouldn't come. Daniel walked on to trackside stock pens. He climbed on the fence and eyed with uncommon sympathy the skinny steers within.

"Sorry-lookin' critters, if ever I saw it," a voice drifted on the chill air as men plodded by on horseback.

"Treaty annuities for the Rosebud," drawled another. "The Sioux dancing for Messiah to come whoop our white hides and what's Uncle Sam do but feed 'em and pet 'em and parcel out goods?"

"All but groomin' them to have a go at us."

"Yes, well, any Injun goes *whoo-whoo* at me is a dead man dancing."

Daniel recalled his father mentioning the "uneasy" mood in the west as homesteaders settled on what had formerly been Indian lands. At the time, it had seemed distant and hazy. But the fear lurking behind the swaggering words of grown men plucked Daniel from the west his father's stories had conjured into the real thing. Grass rustled. But it was only an owl, taking wing from the shadows. He turned back the way he had come to find help in locating his father.

Midway to the depot, men on ponies stirred the dust, approaching. Long braids hung from beneath dark derbies and trailed over blanketed shoulders. Daniel stumbled into a prickly bush and gouged a knuckle, staring after them.

A train rumbled in the station, bell clanging. Sparks flew as it grated to a stop. A handful of passengers got off while others stood to one side, waiting to board. Daniel searched sleepy faces, then veered toward his crate. Its familiar planks were a comfort to his eye.

A boy scrambled atop the mountain of trackside supplies the soldier had been guarding a short while ago. He grinned at Daniel and lifted a friendly hand. "Howdy."

"Howdy," Daniel answered. "You live here?"

"Staying with my uncle for now," said the boy. "How about you?"

"I came on the train from Illinois. Do you know my father, Pierce Tandy?"

"No. Is he supposed to meet you?"

"I didn't tell him I was coming," admitted Daniel.

"He'll likely as not put you on the next train home."

Daniel cocked his head.

"On account of the Sioux," explained the boy. "They're gathering at dance camps and acting crazy. Pa brought Ma and me to town, thinking it would be safer what with the fort close by."

"What's a dance camp?" asked Daniel.

"Kind of a makeshift tent village away from prying eyes. They take their kids out of school and leave their farms and livestock behind and all they do is sing and chant and dance and get all worked up. Pa's afraid they're fixing for an uprising against the whites."

"You mean they're going on the warpath?" asked Daniel.

"Could come to that if the government doesn't hurry up and put some troops on the reservations to settle 'em down." The boy spat on the ground and asked, "Does your pa ranch?"

"No, he's a freighter."

"Out of Valentine?"

Daniel nodded.

"Whereabouts does he live?"

"He's got a cabin between Little White River and the Rosebud Agency."

"That's reservation," said the boy. "Does he haul goods for the Rosebud?"

Daniel shrugged and sucked his pricked knuckle. "All I know is he freights. How would I get there?"

"The Rosebud Agency?" The boy flung an arm in the air, pointing north. "It's thirty miles that away and a little west."

Daniel thanked him and walked on. The sun came up on crowing roosters and dusty streets and houses, some more plainspoken than others. It winked off tin roofs and glazed windows and false fronts. The bacon-grease breeze and a hitching-post full of horses marked the hotel dining room as clearly as the paint-blistered sign.

Daniel found an empty space at a long plank table. A waiter with a bushy face and a soiled apron served him meat and eggs and johnnycakes. The food eased down warm and welcome. But it didn't settle too well on the agitation banging his ears from both sides of the table. Men were piping hot over missing cattle and dance camps and painted Indians. Daniel's neck prickled as they made plans should Indians come sweeping down on ranches and towns with rifles firing.

Thirty miles. That was no stroll across town. Why *was* his father living among the Sioux with trouble brewing and feelings running so high? "Uneasy" was putting it mildly, judging by the fever pitch of these men hunched over plates and coffee cups rehashing a town meeting, and telegrams, letters, and petitions sent to government—state and federal—demanding protection.

Daniel pushed his empty plate aside and reached into his pocket. His hand closed on nothing but the pocketknife. Blood rushed in his eardrums. The din of voices receded. He gaped with burning eyes from the whiskery waiter to a thin-nosed lady collecting money at the door. There was no way out but past her. He made his way there, dragging his feet, his overstuffed stomach tight as a fist.

"That'll be two bits, son," said the woman. Daniel mumbled. She frowned. "What's that? Speak up."

"I left my money at the station." Daniel turned his pockets out so she could see that all he had was a pocketknife.

She sighed. "I'll get the owner."

"I have money," said Daniel. "I'll get it and be right back. I promise."

"Wait here," she called back to him.

Daniel fidgeted and weighed his options as the woman picked her way past the tables to a door and the kitchen beyond. It closed behind her. He bolted out and into the street right into the path of a horse. He dodged it and leaped past a barking dog. Careened into a blanket-draped woman digging through garbage. Frightened a piglet rooting in the dust-choked street.

The baggage and boxes that had surrounded his crate earlier were gone. Daniel flung himself down on the railway platform, reached through the trapdoor, and dragged out the Pony Express saddlebag. But before he could get to his money, the boy he had talked to earlier strode out of the depot and came trotting his way.

"I asked my uncle about your father," the boy said as Daniel rolled to his feet. "Pierce Tandy. Isn't that what you said?" he added, and indicated the bold lettering on the crate.

"The crate's mine," Daniel panted, arms wrapped around the saddlebag.

"I figured it was. Uncle asked these here men to drop it by your pa's and tell him you're here waiting."

Daniel swung toward to see men loading government provisions into heavy wagons. They were leathery Indians in braids and fifty-fifty clothing. Not a white man among them.

"They're hauling sugar, flour, coffee, and cattle out to the Rosebud. It won't be much out of their way," the boy added.

Daniel shifted his gaze to the Winchesters on wagon seats and back to the boy. "Would it be safe to go with them?"

"Reckon you could," the boy said doubtfully. "Though I don't know as I would."

A school bell rang. The boy started away, then

turned and motioned toward the depot. "Go inside and talk to my uncle. He'll tell you what to do."

Daniel eyed the men. The talked in an unfamiliar tongue as they worked. But they seemed pleasant enough. Relaxed. Easy with one another, the way his uncles were when they tackled a job together.

Daniel sucked his tender knuckle, thinking over the boy's suggestion and his earlier words, too. If he did catch a ride with these men, thirty miles was too far for his father to bring him back for the next train home. He was sure of getting to stay at least one night. As he debated, a shout rang out:

"Stop! Stop! Come back here, you little thief!"

Daniel swung around, stuttering an explanation and holding out his saddlebag. But it wasn't the waiter in the greasy apron bearing down on him. Or the narrow-eyed woman. It was an Indian boy, and the piglet he had seen in the street.

Chapter Twenty-two

A red-faced, stubby man in patched jeans and a faded shirt barreled after the boy. "Rotten thievin' Injun. No civilizin' 'em! Don't just stand there, boy. Stop him, stop him!" he roared at Daniel.

Daniel clutched his saddlebags and gawked as the boy spun a quarter turn. His bare feet plowed dust. His long hair slapped skin and bone. He zigged over the tracks, his flour-sack tunic flashing about matchstick legs.

The fiery chuffing engine of a man pounded after him, spewing threats.

The boy zagged back again, pig in arms, and ran straight for the Indian freighters. They had only to stretch out their hands. Instead, they parted. The boy passed through. They closed in, blocking the pig owner's path. He swore and ducked around them.

Daniel dived into his crate while backs were turned and voices raised. "Eyes in the back of her head," Hattie used to say. He had them, too. He could still see them. The hungry boy. The angry man. The iron-jawed Indians with lightning in their night-sky eyes.

He rubbed out the pictures painted on his eyelids. His broken promise, too. He wasn't crawling out again to pay off his two-bit breakfast. Finding his father. That's what mattered. He wouldn't ask for a ride. He would lie still and take it, uninvited.

Daniel's crate was the last thing to be loaded onto the wagon. A whip cracked. The team moved forward. Wheels whined. Freight rubbed shoulders, jostling, creaking, squeaking.

The morning lengthened. The road rocked with creaking wagons and bawling cattle. The dust choked. The sun glared and boiled the air like Earl boiling sap. Daniel eased the trapdoor open. It helped some with the heat, but not the dust. He doused a kerchief in drinking water and tied it about his face.

At midday, the wagon stopped. The team was unhitched into the shade and watered. Daniel looked out as the men ambled off toward a nearby roadhouse. Once they had disappeared inside, he crawled out, drank from the lake, and filled his canteen. Breakfast seemed days ago, the apples very tempting. He pried a crate open with his pocketknife and returned to his box with more than he could eat.

The men returned. They hitched up the teams and pressed on. Late in the afternoon, when the sun cooled, Daniel closed the trapdoor. He closed his eyes, too, and didn't open them again until the wagon reached the Rosebud Agency.

The leftover apples rolled, making a racket as Daniel's crate was lifted to the ground. Dogs sniffed and scratched at his box. People crowded around, talking the same tongue Daniel had been hearing all day. He caught his breath, but no one lifted the lid off his crate.

The freighters must have had help in unloading, for it didn't take long. Daniel and his crate were returned to the wagon. The wagon rolled. The clamor of dogs and feet and voices faded to plodding horses and dusty road and rolling wagon wheels.

The next voice Daniel heard was a child's, followed by more voices. Female. Daniel's belly tipped at a man's low rumble. The tailboard scraped, wood on wood. His crate was slid, then lifted and carried a short distance.

A foot or a breeze caught a door and sent it thudding home on rusty hinges. Thumping hands converged on Daniel's crate. Nails squeaked, wood groaned. The top was lifted away. Daniel sat up.

Alarm leaped in the rust-brown faces of a woman and two girls who must have been the woman's daughters. The girls, one a little younger than Daniel and the other about the age of Anna, gaped at him from eyes a shade lighter than those of the woman.

Daniel ducked their astonished stares and scanned the room. Sparse furnishings. Whitewashed walls. No father. His sinking heart turned over the evidence. It was the freighter's voice he had heard. He had been left at the wrong house! In the yard, wheels were rolling away.

"Catch him! Quick, there's been a mistake!" he cried.

No one moved. Not even an eyelash.

Daniel leaped out of the crate on legs weak as worms. His feet faltered at the door, stopped cold by a picture on the wall. It was Chaldea, falling off her bicycle.

How could that be?

Daniel turned full circle. The walls were covered with his sketches:

Funks Grove crossing. Grampa whittling by the stove. A fence separating grazing cattle from a field of knee-high corn. Gram quilting. Hattie hanging out laundry. Tandy boys spitting watermelon seeds. He recognized something else, too—Gram's Log Cabin quilt. The one she had finished and sent west with the maple candy. It covered a bed.

Daniel swung back to the woman. "Where is my father?"

She touched her ear and then her lips.

"She no longer has ears or tongue for white words," said the older girl.

"You speak English!"

"Yes," said the girl.

"Where is my father?" demanded Daniel.

Her dark gaze flicked over him.

"My father! Pierce Tandy," Daniel said, his voice climbing. "Where is my father?"

A change came over all three faces. The smaller girl clutched her mother's calico skirt. Words whistled through the gap of a missing tooth as she jabbered what sounded like a question. Her mother silenced her with a soft word and a gentle touch. But her gaze went over Daniel like sudden thunder. She spoke what he had come to think of as Indian, and beckoned him closer.

"My mother says have you eating?" said the older girl.

"Where's my father?"

"He has not returned from his job."

"But he lives here?" asked Daniel.

"Yes," said the girl.

"Will he be home tonight?"

The girl translated his question to her mother. The woman responded in the same quiet voice, her expression unchanged.

The girl turned back to Daniel. "Father will come soon."

Days? Hours? Daniel's mind raced, then faltered and backtracked. *Father?* It glared at him, that word.

"My father?"

"*Hau*," said the girl. "I am Julia. This is my mother, and my sister, Magpie. We are happy you are come."

Daniel stared at the girl. She wasn't quite as tall as him. A year, perhaps two, younger. What had dashed through his mind couldn't be. English was not her native tongue. *Your* father. That's what she had meant to say. Maybe her father was a freighter, too. A friend who opened his home to his father. "Is your father a freighter?" he asked.

Julia translated the question for her mother. "Father is a freighter," she replied in turn.

Her hesitation troubled Daniel. He felt behind him for his crate. Sat without thinking. And fell in.

The little one clapped a hand over her giggling mouth. Julia's chin wrinkled. But she didn't laugh. Her mother leaned past her, warning Magpie with a touch and a frowning glance.

Daniel flushed and left rising questions unasked. His thoughts were foolish. As foolish as his legs dangling over the edge of the box. He pulled them in and sat, waiting for someone to make the situation clear to him.

No one did. No one asked why he had come.

Chapter Twenty-three

Julia's mother fried Indian bread. That is what Julia called it when he asked. It smelled like doughnuts cooking. But it wasn't sweet like Hattie's doughnuts. Daniel ate at the table by himself. Fried bread and some chewy meat that tired his teeth and jaws. There was water to drink. The small green leaves floating in it tasted of mint.

Julia and Magpie ate on the floor with their mother. They sat with their legs folded under them, three pairs of calico-draped knees facing the same direction. Daniel felt out of place, sitting alone.

No one talked to him unless he asked a question. Julia paused before answering. Whether she was translating for her mother or answering in her own words, she paused. Just as she had paused when he'd asked if her father was a freighter. Was it to change words in her head from her language to English? Or maybe she didn't want to talk to him.

Sunset faded from the windows as supper was cleared away. Julia lit a lamp. She sat on a folded blanket and shaved a piece of wood with a knife. Her mother slid a leather box from beneath the bed. There was a quilt inside, and a small workbox made from animal skin. She took out the quilt and a thread and needle.

Daniel thought she was preparing to mend the quilt.

But when she shook out the folds, he saw that it was newly made.

"*Wichapi shina.* Star robe," Julia said, touching the quilt.

"Is it for you?" asked Daniel.

"No. For gifting," she said.

"Giving away? My gram does that, too," said Daniel.

"To show belongingness," Julia said, nodding.

Daniel puzzled over her meaning as her mother threaded the needle and began binding the quilt. She sang as she worked. Her tone was low and haunting. It reminded him of Hattie's words about Gram stitching her grief into the cloth.

He took out his sketchbook and pencil.

Dear Gram,

I guess Jack maybe told you by now where I am. I'm at Dad's house, waiting for him to come home. Did you know Indians make quilts? They do. The one I'm seeing has a big star made of lots of colors. Eight points. There are circles and buffalo shapes quilt-stitched in four corners and something else I don't know what in four triangles.

I haven't seen any buffalo yet. Real ones, I mean.

I hope you didn't worry when I was gone. I was thinking I would live with Dad now, if he doesn't care. It will be easier, since Hattie's going to Oklahoma and can't work for us anymore.

If Dad lets me stay, will you send my clothes? There wasn't room in the crate. I'll draw some pictures to send you. I hope you write me a letter soon.

Your grandson, Daniel

Daniel's Story

Daniel made a picture of Julia and her mother, side by side, working with knife and needle. The smoking oil lamp smell burned his eyes and throat. But he finished his sketch and began one of Magpie covering her Indian doll with a scrap of fabric.

Magpie saw him watching her and moving his pencil across the page. She edged close enough to see what he was doing, then returned to her play. By and by, she yawned and put her head in her mother's lap. She was asleep by the time Daniel finished his sketch.

Julia's mother put her sewing away. Daniel sneaked a look at Julia's carving while Julia went outside to shake wood shavings from the blanket. The legs and body of her carving hadn't come out of the wood yet. But he knew by the long nose and flared nostrils that it was to be a horse. He knew, too, who had made the gift horse his father had brought him. He couldn't think why she would send a gift to a boy she didn't know.

"My grandfather used to whittle," Daniel said as Julia returned, folding the blanket.

She looked at him, at his open sketchbook, then took a broom and swept the floor while her mother put Magpie to bed. The broom freshened a scent Daniel had noticed when he had first sat up in the crate. It stung his nose and stirred loneliness, sharp as a knife prick. "What's the smell?" he asked.

"The river is not far, if you wish to bathe," replied Julia.

Daniel flushed. He *did* need a bath. But that wasn't what he smelled. Whatever the scent was, it took his thoughts home with every sting.

Julia's mother slid a leather box like her sewing box from beneath the bed. She unlaced it and gave Daniel a flour-sack shirt and a towel made of the same coarse fabric.

Julia retrieved soap from the washbasin and the smoking lamp from the table and lighted his way along a weedy path. Clouds skirted the dark sky. Underbrush rustled. An owl hooted. Coyotes' yips filled the night. It seemed to Daniel some distance before he heard water licking the night shore.

Julia showed him a shallow, sandy place to go into the water.

Afraid he might lose his way in the dark, Daniel said, "Wait for me on the path, okay? It won't take me long."

She retreated, lantern in hand.

Daniel crouched, shivering in the dark, cold water, rubbing soap into his stiff hair and over his body. He soaped and rinsed his shirt and trousers and stockings and union suit before leaving the water. The flour-sack shirt fell past his knees. He slipped his feet into his shoes. Hearing a drumming sound in the distance, he called to Julia, "Do you hear something?"

"It is tom-toms," said Julia. "They dance for Messiah's return."

"You mean the Ghost Dance?" Daniel broke out in goose bumps. He stumbled up the bank and down the path to where Julia was seated on the ground with the flickering lamp. "Where?" he kept his voice down.

"On the flats upriver," she said.

The beating drums freshened the suspicion, agitation, and anger Daniel had witnessed in Valentine. His thoughts skipped from the boy at the station to the men in the restaurant to the swift fire in the eyes of Indian freighters.

The lantern lighted Julia's face as she rose beside him. Her face was somber, but calm. Reassured by her lack of fear, Daniel got a grip on his own nervous jitters and asked, "Do boys and girls dance, too? Or just the grown-ups?"

"I will rub the soap into your clothes," she said, ignoring his question.

"I already washed them," said Daniel. "How far is it to where they're dancing?"

She paused. "It is not far."

"Have you been?"

"My father fears the dancing will bring soldiers and trouble."

Her failure to give a direct answer quickened Daniel's curiosity. "We won't dance. We'll just look," he reasoned. "You want to?"

Just when Daniel thought Julia would refuse, she put out the lamp. He dropped his wet clothes beside it and trotted along the riverbank at her heels. By and by, he saw the light of a campfire on a flat piece of ground on the other side of the river. Julia dropped to her knees on the parched ground. Daniel hunkered beside her and peered across the waters.

Smoke and whirling dust hung in a cloud over the tents encircling the campfire. Firelight sketched eerie shadows on the canvas walls as men, women, and children joined hands and moved their feet and swayed forward on bent knees.

Daniel's ears, his eyes, his skin pulsed with the drumming feet and drumming tom-toms and his own drumming heart. His pulse reeled at a small rustling in the parched grass. Julia heard it, too. Silent, motionless and alert, she reminded him of a deer in thick timber, head up, poised to bolt and run. Had she done so, Daniel would have followed. But she didn't run. Apparently she was satisfied it was only the breeze. She faced the river again and watched dancers circle inside circles. The circles blurred in the darkness and the firelit dust. Daniel couldn't take his eyes off the dizzying dance. The chanting voices rose in intensity. "What are they saying?" he asked in a whisper.

Julia translated the words into English in a hushed and rhythmic voice:

"'Someone cometh to tell news, to tell news,
There shall be a buffalo chase.
Make arrows. Make arrows.
The people are coming home,
Saith my father, saith my father.'"

Words like "cometh" and "saith" put Daniel in mind of Sunday mornings in the white-framed Funks Grove Church with its double aisles and twin doors and tall windows letting in sunlight. "Preacher talk," Jack called it. The dancers bent their knees deeper. Their chants grew louder, the drums stronger until all sound melded in Daniel's ears like pulsing throbs. Shadows fell from the tent walls as dancers collapsed in the dust.

"Some who fall to the ground are caught up to the Land of Deceased Relatives," murmured Julia.

Daniel flinched, thinking of Grampa Silas. "You mean they *die?*"

"No. They visit relations who have gone before and return with news of the Messiah with nail prints in his hands. He came long ago. The rascally *wasicus* treated him badly. Soon he comes for his Indian children."

Wasicus. Daniel wondered who that might be. He thought about his father's visit last spring when he had first learned of the Ghost Dance religion and of the games he and Anna and Jack had played. "What about the rest of us? Will he come for us, too?" he asked the question Jack had asked that night.

Julia picked up a stick and looked away from him. "Those who do not dance, my mother says, the dirt will cover over."

"Enough dirt to kill us?"

"*Hau.*" The single word fell soft and forlorn, like wind-stirred ash.

Daniel shivered. "Does your mother dance? Do *you?*"

"I have not," she said. "Father does not wish me to."

"He must not believe it, then."

"Father does not believe the time of His coming is known," she confirmed.

"What about you?" asked Daniel.

"I do not know."

Daniel rubbed an itching ear and watched the dance and listened to the chants floating across the river on the chilly night air.

"My mother says the time cometh, I shall see Him. The time cometh, Mother says," said Julia softly.

Daniel knew she was translating, and still he turned and looked over his shoulder. Julia swung around, too. "Mother must not be looking for us here."

"She'll tell your father?" asked Daniel.

Julia lowered her gaze to the ground. "No. She would not tell him."

Puzzled at her broken whisper, Daniel waited for her to explain. Instead, she rubbed her stick through the sand, then laid it aside with such care, it might have been a living thing. "Come," she said finally. "We must go back."

Chapter Twenty-four

Daniel hung his wet clothes over the fence. When he went inside, Julia had gone to bed with her mother and Magpie. Daniel put out the lamp and crawled into the other bed. He covered himself with Gram Tandy's Log Cabin quilt and curled on his side. Two beds were not enough for two men, two children, and a woman. Or was it only one man? Did only four people live in this house?

"He took his grief west." That was all that was ever said about his father going away. Daniel had accepted it as true. Now he faced the tattered blanket separating the two beds. And wondered.

Daniel knew the year his father had returned to Illinois and married his mother. It was the year before his birth. He didn't know Julia's age, just that she was a little younger than him. If she *was* his father's daughter, his father had not grieved for long.

Tomorrow, he would come out and ask who was who and what was what and learn why his father was living here.

Daniel awoke to find Magpie in his crate, rolling an apple between her hands. He swung his feet to the floor. Magpie blinked in the gray light and put the apple down.

He fumbled for his pocketknife, then crouched beside the crate in his flour-sack nightshirt, peeled the apple, and held it out to Magpie. She looked at it a long moment before taking it.

Julia and her mother were still in bed. By the time Daniel had cleaned the ashes from the stove, he realized they were waiting for him to leave so they could dress. He picked up the bucket. At the door, he turned back and motioned to Magpie. She followed him into the crisp September dawn, and around the back of the weathered cabin, eating her apple.

"Did my father tell you about me?" Daniel asked her.

"Boy-who-makes-pictures," Magpie strung the words together like a hyphenated name.

"He didn't tell me about you," said Daniel.

She frowned and rubbed her toe in the dirt. "Your sister cannot make pictures."

"You mean *you? You're* my sister?" Daniel asked, pointing.

"*Hau.*"

Did that mean "yes"? Daniel thought so, but wasn't sure. He squinted at Magpie, looking for clues. Her eyes didn't seem as dark as they had seemed inside. Neither was her hair. It curled a little at the ends, and she had a freckle over her lip. *Or was it a mole?* His father had a mole on his lip, too.

He dumped the ashes on the garden patch. The ground was cracked and dry. Nothing grew there but tangled weeds and withered vines. *Sister, sister, sister,* the wind whistled through them.

"Is Julia my sister, too?" he asked Magpie.

"*Hau.*"

"That means 'yes,' right?"

"*Hau,*" she said again.

Daniel pulled his clothes off the fence and ducked into the privy to dress. When he came out again, Magpie was sitting on the woodpile. There was a hatchet in the chopping block. Splitting kindling wasn't a chore he did at home. But it felt good to break something. He stopped and sucked his sore knuckle and chopped some more.

Julia came around back.

He looked at her and asked, "Why didn't you tell me?"

"Tell you what?"

"That you and Magpie are my sisters."

"It is not for me to name your relatives," she replied.

"It's true, then?" he asked.

"Father will tell you when he comes," she said.

"He never did before," said Daniel.

Julia spoke to Magpie in their native tongue. Magpie's reply had a whine in it. It was not her fault. She didn't deserve a scolding. Daniel shut his mouth and said no more.

Julia caught Magpie's hand. Together, they went to milk a cow and care for the horses. Daniel finished what he had begun, then went inside with an armload of kindling and stove wood.

After breakfast, Julia's mother spoke to him, but not in English.

"Mother will tend your hurt hand," Julia translated.

"It's just a splinter," said Daniel. He suspected by the flicker in her eye that Julia's mother understood him, but she reached for his hand as if he had not protested, and probed his knuckle with a needle. The broken tip of the thorn came out at her prodding. She mixed a herbal potion that put Daniel strongly in mind of Chaldea. Something else fell in place, too. The stinging scent that took him home—it was sage.

"What is your mother's name?" Daniel asked Julia when her mother had finished.

"Sweet Grass," Julia replied.

Daniel hoped Sweet Grass wasn't a hexer. He thanked her and gave her the last of his apples just in case. When Julia went outside, he followed. The pasture, like the yard and garden, was weedy and beaten down, tinder waiting for a spark. Daniel watched Julia hitch a team of lean horses to a light wagon. "Are you going somewhere?" Daniel asked.

"It is annuity day," she said. "We go there now to collect our rations."

"To Rosebud? Can I mail a letter there?"

"If you wish," said Julia.

Daniel raced inside and got the letter he had written to Gram. Sweet Grass and Magpie followed him out. Magpie scrambled up on the wagon seat. Sweet Grass spoke to Daniel and motioned for him to get in, too.

He climbed in the back, leaving the seat for Sweet Grass and his half sisters.

Chapter Twenty-five

Heaping white clouds threw shadows over the parched and wind-scrubbed country. Wild grasses whispered beneath the wagon wheels like wind blowing through Chaldea's remedy basket. Blackbirds swooped from the sky, eating the insects the horses and wagon stirred. There was little to be harvested within the scorched fields they passed. Even the livestock looked shriveled and thin and listless.

"The earth is our mother. Growing crops in her lap is new to the Dakota," Julia said when Daniel mentioned the fertile farms back home. "They like better growing the spotted buffalo."

"Cattle, you mean?"

She nodded. "Rain is needed for the grasses to make them fat."

The Sioux, Daniel knew, were also called Teton Dakota, and Lakota. Sweet Grass, he learned, belonged to the Brulé tribe of the Sioux. Rosebud Reservation was the land appointed to the Brulé bands, and where they gathered for biweekly rations. As they rode along, Sweet Grass spoke through Julia of bygone days when her people had followed the buffalo across the plains. In the deep winters they had sheltered in the Black Hills. *Paha Sapa*, Julia called it. She said it was their holy land, and sacred to the Sioux. Sweet Grass's voice softened when she spoke of it. When Daniel asked a question, she sometimes responded before Julia finished translating.

The Rosebud Agency, when they reached it, was a town unto itself with an Indian camp at the outskirts. Everywhere Daniel looked there were canvas tents and cooking fires and ponies and people milling about.

"Our people were counted last year, and rations were cut. Now they fall short and some go hungry. We are happy for the day to collect our food," Julia told him. She went on to explain that many families had traveled a long distance. They camped and visited and played games while they waited for the agent to release their rations.

Sweet Grass sought out her relatives and climbed down to visit. Daniel helped Julia secure the wagon while Magpie raced off to join some friends. Men visited in clusters. Women grouped about cooking pots or sat in the shade with needlework.

As Julia led the way through the camp, Daniel saw how intently the grown-ups talked with one another. He noticed gleaming eyes and mouths that flattened, then crimped, and teeth that flashed as they poured out words. "What's all the excitement? What're they talking about?" he asked Julia.

"The Messiah Dance," she replied.

"The dancers are here?"

"They have come for their rations. They speak of journeys to the Spirit world."

Daniel's Story

Julia returned to her mother. Sweet Grass sat with her knees to one side, looking on as a woman painted symbols on a shirt. Their conversation appeared earnest.

"My mother's sister makes ghost shirts for herself and her children," said Julia.

Daniel paused beside her and watched Sweet Grass's sister dip a bone brush into a turtle shell containing red paint.

"Come, we will mail your letter," Julia said after a moment.

"What's a ghost shirt?" Daniel asked as they walked on.

"The dancers now wear them," said Julia. "One of our men has said such shirts have power over bullets. If the bluecoats come, their bullets will fall harmlessly to the ground."

"You mean soldiers?" Puzzled, Daniel said, "Soldiers don't go around shooting women and children. They don't shoot anybody, unless it's war."

A clamor in the camp cut Daniel short. Men and women young and old scrambled to their feet. Children abandoned their games and darted after their parents. Their words fell meaningless on his ears, but he saw Julia's eyes widen and caught her fear. "What is it?" he cried.

"Bluecoats are coming! Where is Magpie?"

Daniel pivoted in the whirling dust and confusion, looking. Failing to find her, he lurched after Julia as if in a dream. Women raced past with frightened children. Ponies strained at picket lines. Men dived into tents fully dressed and out in breech cloths with their faces painted. They leaped on pawing ponies and galloped away with their weapons aloft.

"What's happened?" gasped Daniel. "Where are they going?"

"They ride to cut off the bluecoats, so that we may have time to hide ourselves. Come! Mother will hitch the team. We must find Magpie and flee!"

Heart in his throat, Daniel stumbled after Julia, bleating Magpie's name into the dust-choked air. They found her hiding in the grass with some friends. He caught her small hand in his.

"Hurry!" Julia raced ahead, leading the way through the pandemonium to the horses.

Sweet Grass was waiting in the wagon. Her strained face and the urgency in her motioning arms broke the language barrier. Daniel clambered up after the girls. As they were pulling away, a young man rode southward after the Indians.

"Agent Wright," Julia said as the man galloped out the gate.

"Where's he going?" Daniel panted, his chest hurting.

Sweet Grass responded in her own tongue.

"He rides after our men," Julia put her mother's words into English. "Mother says he will turn our men back if he can. It is his duty to keep the peace. He does not wish our people to fight the bluecoats."

"But why would soldiers come here?" cried Daniel.

"They have come to punish those who dance the Ghost Dance," said Julia gravely.

✳

Daniel's Story

The trip home was swift and somber and edgy. Daniel climbed down, his letter still in his pocket. He helped Julia with the team. Sweet Grass hurried them along. Once inside the cabin, she wouldn't let them go out again. She was fearful of the soldiers and anxious for news. None came. Nor did Daniel's father.

They ate a cold supper. Afterward, Daniel trimmed the wick and cleaned the chimney lamp. Sweet Grass took out her sewing workbox. Her hand paused, and her face tightened each time the wind whistled or the lamp caught a draft, making the flame flicker on the white-washed walls and Daniel's drawings.

Julia frowned over her carving.

Daniel took out his sketchbook, but couldn't concentrate for the trapped, smothery feeling within. It caught at his throat like the air of the sod box on the dusty road coming here. He returned his sketchbook to his saddlebag and took out the small box Jack had given him. He slipped his finger through the hole in the bottom and folded it onto the bed of cotton. "Look here, Magpie," he said, lifting off the lid. "My sore finger fell off."

She jumped, then giggled when he wiggled his finger. Julia liked the joke, too.

Even Sweet Grass smiled. Magpie crawled into Daniel's crate to see if there were more jokes inside.

Daniel tore up little paper scraps for tickets and tried to hold the darkness back by teaching Anna's game of train to Magpie.

"All aboard!" he called. "Next stop, Pittsburgh!"

Magpie giggled and repeated his words. Daniel chuffed

and chooed and pushed the crate across the wooden floor. Across and back, across and back until bedtime.

An old Indian gentleman came at daybreak with news that yesterday's rumor was false. There were no soldiers en route to the agency to punish Ghost Dancers. Agent Wright, he said, had overtaken the armed band of Brulé who had ridden out yesterday and convinced them they had been misinformed. After being reassured that their lives and those of their families were not in danger, the Brulé men had returned to the Rosebud Agency with Mr. Wright. Now Agent Wright wanted those who had scattered to reassemble at the agency today so that he could talk with them.

Sweet Grass served Indian hash for breakfast. *Wasna*, Julia called it. The meat was dried; the berries, too. Daniel could taste grease and sugar mixed in. Sweet Grass divided the hash they didn't eat among a dish on the table, an animal skin, and the elderly messenger who went on his way. After they had eaten, she gave Julia the animal-skin container. Daniel followed Julia outside. She stowed the food under the wagon seat and hitched up the team.

"We will listen to the agent and collect our rations," Julia said when Daniel asked.

Daniel went inside to get the letter he had yet to mail. Sweet Grass shooed Magpie out the door after him. They climbed into the wagon. Sweet Grass motioned to Daniel. "Mother wishes you to stay behind. Someone must look after the animals," explained Julia.

Daniel's Story

Daniel climbed down, ears burning. Sweet Grass took the lines in hand and spoke to the team. The horses responded and trotted out the lane, leaving him behind.

At first, Daniel assumed they would be home by nightfall. But as he was caring for the animals that evening, he recalled Julia's words and realized that Sweet Grass had anticipated being gone overnight.

Horses passed in the night, but they did not stop.

Daniel got up and ate the last of the Indian hash from the dish Sweet Grass had left behind. By noon, he was hungry again. He eyed the apples, still on the table. He had given them to Sweet Grass and it didn't seem right to eat them. So he went to the river to fish. Dust rose from the direction of the dance camp.

The fish were not biting. Daniel set several bank poles, then walked upriver. The drums sounded angry. He turned back, collected his poles, and returned to the cabin without any fish.

There was flour and baking powder and fresh milk from the cow. He mixed it together the way Hattie did for pancakes and boiled sugar and water for syrup. Without eggs, it didn't hold together so well. But the emptiness in his belly went away.

The night was full of creaks and bumps and whispery sounds. Daniel gave up trying to sleep. He climbed out of bed, put the lid on his crate, and crawled inside wrapped in Gram's Log Cabin quilt.

His father came home in the morning and found him there.

Chapter Twenty-six

Daniel's father wasn't as surprised as he might have been. He had arrived in Valentine to find letters and telegrams from home waiting for him.

"They're worried sick back home," said his father. "What do you mean, taking off like that and not telling anyone?"

"I told Jack," Daniel said, shuffling his feet.

"You did? Then why didn't he tell Harmony?"

"It wasn't his fault. Tandys don't tell on—"

"Don't start that with me," his father cut in. He flung his dusty hat and coat down on the crate Daniel had just crawled out of. "Wasn't bad enough Harmony's grieving over Father, you pull a stunt like this. The whole countryside's looking. Including Matthew and Hattie, who should be on their way to Oklahoma but aren't because of you. I declare, I'd tan your hide if I wasn't so relieved to see you. Who was the know-nothing who sold you the ticket?" Pierce's teeth glimmered in his dusty face.

"Jack tried, but they wouldn't sell it to him," Daniel admitted in a whisper.

"Then how did you get here?"

Daniel rubbed his prickly nose and pointed to the crate.

Amazement broke through Pierce's anger. "You came in a *box*? Whose fool idea was that?"

Daniel hung his head and didn't answer.

His father crossed to the stove and rattled the empty coffee pot. "How'd you find the cabin?" he asked.

Daniel explained about the trapdoor and the freighters delivering him.

"Must have given Sweet Grass and the girls a jolt."

"I was surprised, too," Daniel said in a small voice.

The heat left Pierce's eyes and stained his cheeks. He drew a hand over his sagging face and turned his attention to soap and water.

Able to breathe again, Daniel trailed him to the washbasin. He rubbed a gash on the floor with the toe of his shoe and slid his father a sidelong glance. "They didn't like me at first."

Pierce swung around. "What makes you say that?"

"They made me sit at the table alone while they ate on the floor."

"You were their guest. They were honoring your custom."

"What custom?"

"Eating at the table. I suppose you thought everyone did."

Daniel's ears prickled at his tone. "They wouldn't talk to me, either. Unless I asked a question. Then Julia answered. She paused a long, long time, like she really didn't want to."

"Thought comes before speech. It's good etiquette

among the Sioux," said his father. He splashed his hands and face and reached for a flour-sack towel.

"Do they know about Grampa dying?" Daniel asked meekly. "Because they didn't ask about him or Gram, either."

"Julia carved the horse to honor Father's memory. Sweet Grass helped Magpie make the rider." His father spread the towel over a chair back with a calloused hand. "As for them not asking about your gram, Sweet Grass isn't prone to firing off questions. She thinks it's a sign of poor breeding."

Daniel thought over the questions he had asked. He shifted his feet, hoping he hadn't disgraced anyone. "No one told me."

"Now you know," said his father. He stretched out a weathered hand. "Come here and let me get a good look at you. Twelve hundred miles in a box. You're getting taller, but I'm not sure you're getting any smarter." He wagged his head in resignation and embraced him roughly.

Eyes stinging, Daniel hid his face against his father's frayed and faded shirt. "Dad? About the girls—"

"We'll talk about it later," his father cut him short. "I bought groceries while I was in town. I could use some help carrying them in."

"Sure. I'll help," said Daniel.

His father clapped him on the shoulder and let him go. Daniel helped put the supplies away. Glad he wasn't Lakota, and restricted by good manners from asking questions, he asked where Sweet Grass was going to store her rations. And what she needed with them now that the shelves were crowded with staples.

"Her people were promised annuities when they gave up their land," his father explained. "It is owed to them. What she doesn't use, she shares with others who need it." He moved to the window overlooking the fenced-in pasture. "I figured they would be back from Rosebud by now."

"They went once, but they had to go back," said Daniel. "Somebody said soldiers were coming. We found out later it wasn't true, but they believed it at the time. The men grabbed their guns and jumped on their ponies and rode off. Sweet Grass was scared, so we came home."

"I heard about it in Valentine," said his father. He poured beans into the coffee grinder and turned the handle. "You shouldn't have come here, Daniel."

"I want to live with you," protested Daniel.

"You can't right now. It isn't safe. You saw how the threat of soldiers alarmed the Indians. The homesteaders are just as fearful of soldiers *not* being sent. Why do you think Sweet Grass left you behind? Feelings are running high. She doesn't know what to expect from the agent, or how her people will react."

"You know about that, too?"

"Agent Wright calling the Brulés in? Yes. I know."

"You could come home," said Daniel.

"And leave my family behind with rumors on both sides flying like sparks and the whole countryside a tinderbox?"

Family. Daniel felt the injury of all the years he had

waited. He sniffed and wiped his nose on his sleeve and shuffled his feet. "They could come, too," he said finally.

"This is Sweet Grass's home. Her people. She doesn't want to go, and I don't want to rock the boat, pressing her when we're already at odds over this Ghost Dance business."

Then let her stay, Daniel thought. But something in his father's weary eyes kept him from saying it.

His father fixed breakfast. They ate and cleared it away. Sweet Grass and the girls still hadn't returned.

"I have to ride to Rosebud and wire Harmony that you're safe," said his father. "If the agent is through with his powwow, we'll all come home together."

His father looked like he hadn't slept in a while. Daniel didn't bother asking if he could ride along. Faced again with more time to kill, he went to the river to see if the Ghost Dancers had returned to their camp.

From the sandy riverbank, Daniel saw the circle of tents. It didn't look as large as it had seemed when he had come here with Julia. The tom-toms were silent. There was no singing or dancing. People were moving about in an unhurried fashion, much like they had at the agency before the soldier rumor raced through the camp.

Daniel returned to the house for his sketchbook, then forded the river for a better view and hid himself in tall grasses. He was still too far away to make out the faces of the people or the details of their clothing. In his drawing, he clad them in leggings and moccasins, and ghost shirts like the one he had seen Sweet Grass's sister making at the agency camp.

The sights and sounds of nature retreated as Daniel's hand raced over the page. At length he paused to rest his cramped finger. He heard sand shift underfoot to his left. He swung around, glimpsed a painted face, and leaped for the river.

Chapter Twenty-seven

Daniel was wet to the knees before he recognized Julia's voice. He climbed out, chilled and feeling foolish. "I didn't know it was you."

"I was coming to see is Father come home," said Julia.

"He came, but he left again. He had to send Gram a telegram," Daniel said, water squishing in his shoes. "He didn't find you?"

"We have not seen him."

"I don't know how you missed him. He was going straight to the agency and back." Daniel stared at red circles, crescents, and crosses painted on her forehead, chin, and cheeks. "Why'd you paint your face?"

Julia indicated with an uplifted hand the flats before them.

Daniel's jaw dropped. "You've been up there? All day?"

"My mother joins the dancers," said Julia. Eyes downcast, she added, "It will displease my father."

"Then what'd she do it for?" asked Daniel.

"Last year when rumors of the coming Messiah reached the ears of our people, men were chosen to journey to the desert in search of the truth. My mother's relative Short Bull was among those chosen," explained

Julia. "Short Bull returned with news of the one they call Wovoka. Wovoka's power, he says, is great. He puts the sun in the sea, making the waters boil. When my mother tells Father of her relative's word, he is indignant. 'The sun does not set in the sea.' He gives with two round stones a lesson of the earth and the sun. Wovoka, he says, is not the Messiah."

"Messiah?" Daniel said, startled. "I thought he was a prophet."

"Some now believe him to be the Messiah spoken of in the holy book." Voice dropping to a whisper, she admitted, "I do not know if it is so. But what can be so wrong to dance? It gives hope."

Julia's painted face both chilled and intrigued Daniel. But her dilemma and her unhappiness over it made his stomach hurt. Feeling exposed and increasingly uneasy, he gathered his pencils and the sketchbook. "I'm going back to the cabin. Are you coming?" he asked.

Julia moved forward a step, then stopped. The sound of tom-toms lifted on the dry, dusty day. She glanced back toward the flats. Tears rose in her eyes. "What if Father is mistaken? Will Great Messiah cover me over if I do not dance?" she asked in a torn voice.

Daniel thought about all the stories Jack had told of Chaldea being a witch, and talking to the dead and such, and how it gave him the chills, even when Hattie reassured him none of it was true. "Tell him you're scared not to," said Daniel.

The cross on Julia's chin quivered as she wrestled

with her decision. She drew a hand over her painted cheek and turned away. Daniel watched her retreat through the weeds and turned homeward.

Once at the cabin, Daniel changed into the flour-sack shirt and hung his clothes by the stove. They were nearly dry when his father returned. He told him where his "family" was.

His father's alarm hardened to a grimness Daniel had not seen in him before. Daniel was certain he would go storming after them. Instead, Pierce drew a hand over his trail-battered face, kicked off his boots, turned back the quilt, and stretched out on the bed. Daniel's ears tingled, waiting for him to speak. But he just lay there, his hand locked behind his head, staring at the ceiling.

"Will they come home for supper?" Daniel asked when the silence was too heavy to bear.

"If they get hungry enough," said his father. "Agent Wright sent all the Brulé home without their rations. He told them to think it over and make up their minds what is right: to dance or to eat."

Daniel frowned and rubbed his own half-empty belly. "That's mean," he said at length.

"It's an ugly tool for getting the upper hand. But it works more often than not."

"I'd let them have their food," said Daniel. "Let them dance, too. What's it hurt?"

"Not everyone feels that way. Homesteaders fear the dancing will lead to open rebellion. Town folk, too. They're all up in arms and demanding action," his father went over it again, then closed his weary eyes and turned his face to the wall, ending the conversation.

Daniel went outside and sat on the rail fence. The drums played in the distance. Dust lifted from the dance camp. Was Julia bending her knees now? Chanting the chants?

It was a long while before Daniel smelled supper cooking and went inside. His father had fixed meat and fried potatoes and gravy. Daniel was mopping up the last of his gravy with a biscuit when Sweet Grass and the girls came in on soundless feet.

Pierce looked from their painted faces to the ghost shirt Sweet Grass was wearing. His mouth jerked into a flat, white line. He placed his weathered hands palms down on the table, elbows bent, and scraped back his chair. He hesitated endlessly in that half-standing position. "Have you girls eaten supper?" he finally asked, and the room breathed again.

"No, Father," Julia said in a whisper.

"There's food on the stove," said Pierce.

Sweet Grass spoke in her quiet voice and went out. Pierce followed.

"Where's she going?" whispered Daniel.

If Julia heard him, she didn't answer. Daniel watched her fill a plate for herself and Magpie.

"You can have my chair," he said, and got up, making room at the table.

But she sat on the floor as before. Magpie did the same.

Daniel crossed to the window overlooking the

backyard and pasture. His father was unhitching the team. Sweet Grass was sitting on the ground near the woodpile. She faced the cabin, her back to his father. *Was their talk over with that quickly?*

Julia put her food aside and joined Daniel at the window. "She comes to collect our belongings and tell Father she will not be living with a white man anymore," she said in a low voice.

"Just because he doesn't want her to dance?"

Julia said nothing.

"What about you and Magpie?" Daniel pressed for an answer.

"We will stay at the dance camp."

"You're dancing, then?"

Julia turned her eyes away. A tear escaped and slid down her cheek. She moved from the window and sat down again with Magpie.

Daniel looked out over the yard and saw his father cross to the woodpile. He couldn't hear what he was saying to Sweet Grass. But looking on gave Daniel the same feeling he'd had the day he had learned of Grampa's accident and no one would say the word "dead."

After a while, his father returned to the house. Sweet Grass followed. Had the cabin sprouted inside walls with rooms to separate, the silence they kept could not have been deeper or the distance wider.

Sweet Grass took out her sewing widgets and muslin, the kind Gram used for quilt backing. She cut from it two shapeless garments, smaller versions of the one she was wearing. Daniel saw they were to be ghost shirts. His father must have guessed it, too. It was bedtime when he took Magpie and Julia to one side.

"Your mother wants you to go with her tomorrow and join the dancing," he said, his voice falling into the silent room as flat and colorless as the cloth Sweet Grass was stitching. "I'd forbid it, but what's that mean to her? She'll just do like she did today and slip off with you first chance she gets."

The hard resignation in his voice sent Magpie across the room and into her mother's arms. Watching Julia, Pierce asked, "How about you? What do you want to do?"

Julia tucked her chin.

Seeing her mouth quiver and a tear fall unchecked, Daniel spoke up, saying, "She's scared that if she doesn't dance, the Messiah will come and cover her with dirt."

"I've told you before Wovoka is *not* the Messiah, Julia," Pierce said in a tone of studied patience. "If he were, he wouldn't be claiming information that nobody but God Himself knows."

Julia didn't answer.

Pierce took a Bible from a crude wooden shelf. "Your grandmother, the one you're named for, taught me how to read using this book," he continued in the same taut, velvet-over-flint voice. "The Sioux learned of the Messiah through preaching from this same book. About Him dying on the Cross and how the grave couldn't hold Him and how He promised to come back to Earth someday for those who believe in Him. You know all this, and so does your mother. But the part that keeps getting past her ears is where Jesus warns people against anyone who claims to know *when* He's coming again. Here, read for yourself what He says," he said to Julia.

Julia wiped her eyes with the back of her hand and took a chair at the table. The room was quiet except for Pierce turning pages and adjusting the lantern. Daniel shifted away from the stove and looked on over Julia's shoulder as she moved her finger across the line, silently tracking words.

"Out loud, so your mother understands I'm not the one twisting words," Pierce said without looking Sweet Grass's way.

"'Then if any man shall say unto you, Lo, here is Christ, or there; believe it not. For there shall arise false Christs, and false prophets, and shall shew great signs and wonders; insomuch that, if it were possible, they shall deceive the very elect.'"

Reading the words to himself as Julia translated them for her mother, Daniel thought about the sun setting in the sea. He had never seen the sea. But back home, when the sun slipped behind autumn trees, the leaves looked like flames. If it was the first you had seen the sun setting behind trees, a trickster might scare you, shouting, "Fire!"

"'Behold, I have told you before. Wherefore if they shall say unto you, Behold, he is in the desert; go not forth: behold, he is in the secret chambers; believe it not. For as the lightning cometh out of the east and shineth even unto the west; so shall also the coming of the Son of man be.'"

Julia lifted her eye from the page. "What is 'elect'?" she asked.

"The Messiah's followers, those who are watching and waiting for Him," said Pierce. He looked directly at Sweet Grass, then added, "Like your mother. Except she's been deceived by add-on words that sound good to her ears."

Sweet Grass paused in holding the garment she had cut against Magpie's small frame for sizing. His father rose from the table and crossed to where she sat with Magpie's face buried against her. "He didn't say sew a magic shirt, dance, and I'll come for you in the spring of ninety-one," he said, his shadow looming over her in the flickering lamplight. "He said don't go on a wild goosechase looking. He *said* when He comes, it will be as clear as lightning sweeping over the sky."

"For this wisdom I should stay with a white man and be made foolish before the eyes of my daughters?" Sweet Grass replied in hushed intonations of near-perfect English.

"I'm not trying to make you look foolish. I'm telling you you can't mix truth and deception like fifty-fifty clothes. The whole countryside is groaning under the burden of change, and to the whites, this dancing is warlike."

"What foolishness!" Sweet Grass scoffed, hands moving protectively over Magpie's quivering shoulders. "Do women and children dance War Dances?"

"You and I know they don't. But folks with itchy

trigger fingers may not be persuaded by the government's wait-and-see attitude. And no matter what you've been told, these shirts won't stop bullets," he said, and reached as if to take the shirts.

Swiftly, Sweet Grass thrust her sewing behind her. She spoke to Julia. Responding, Julia came to her side and urged Magpie out of her mother's lap and to her feet. They slipped silently past their father and out the door without looking his way.

"Don't leave the yard," Pierce called after them.

Daniel's nerves gathered in knots as he waited for a dismissal that never came. Hunkered down before the woman who didn't want him anymore, his father had forgotten him.

"I know you're trying to find your way back to the old red road. It's understandable. Just as you know the ways of your people, I know mine. I'm afraid for you, Sweet Grass, and I'm afraid for the girls," Pierce said with splinters in his voice.

"It would not be good for my daughters if Messiah comes and we have not danced," she replied.

"The real Messiah sees hearts. Whether or not you dance, He knows that yours is good toward Him," reasoned Pierce.

"Perhaps if you dance, He will forgive the unkindness shown Him by your people in the past," said Sweet Grass. "Perhaps He will not cover you over when He comes for his Indian children."

"I'm telling you, His judgment isn't by the skin, it's by the heart," said Pierce. "Why won't you listen?"

Daniel's Story

The anger his words provoked was as visible as the lightning of which he had spoken. It found open sky in Sweet Grass's dark eyes and in the mockery of her soft voice: "These rough words you speak to the mother of your daughters—these come from your good heart?"

"You won't listen to words written from Messiah's own mouth and you won't listen to me. Fine!" Pierce said with an impatient gesture. "But if you take these girls, and any harm comes to them, it's on your head. Remember that, you hear?"

In returning the Bible to the shelf, Pierce's gaze fell on Daniel, still at the table. A muscle in his leathered cheek twitched. But he didn't acknowledge him. Instead, he strode out the door and closed it on air still sharp with his words. Alone with Sweet Grass, Daniel squirmed in his chair. His chest felt as if it would explode, so tight was the breath he was holding. He let it go slowly, took off his shoes, and crawled into bed fully dressed.

Only then did Sweet Grass rise from her place. She moved the tattered blanket in place as a curtain between the two beds, then called in the girls.

Daniel pulled Gram's Log Cabin quilt over his head. He heard the sound of his father in the yard splitting stove wood with nothing but moon and stars to guide the strokes of the hatchet. Recalling that only a few days ago he, too, had needed to break things, he buried his head in his arms and tried to stop his insides from shaking.

It was a long while before his father came inside. Daniel wasn't used to sharing a bed. His father's restless tossing and the echo of words that had flown like dirt from the dirt box the day Jack emptied it on Anna kept him awake. He remembered Earl getting caught in the spray. But it was only dirt. Earl was big and tough and not a bit scared of it burying him. And to Anna, it was only a game.

When Daniel finally fell asleep, he slept so soundly that he would have missed the girls' departure if not for Sweet Grass. She placed the folded quilt she had made on the foot of his bed and spoke words he didn't understand. He rubbed the sleep from his eyes and saw Julia, fully dressed and wrapped in a blanket.

"For your grandmother," Julia put her mother's words in English.

There were no tears today. No paint, either. Julia's face was without expression, like a cloud shadow that passes over a field.

Sweet Grass led Magpie out by the hand. Julia followed. Daniel stumbled to the door. His father walked toward the river with the girls in the cold, damp gray before dawn. They led a pack pony. Sweet Grass trailed some distance behind, leading a second pack pony.

Daniel chewed the cuff of his shirtsleeve and watched until he could see them no more. His father would not leave him. He would be back. He knew this. Yet the cold, hard knot in his gut remained.

It was a long while before Pierce returned. Daniel's numb toes curled away from the cabin floor. He perched on the bed and hugged his bent knees to his chest. His father crossed to the stove with an armload of wood. He shook the ashes from the grate. It hurt Daniel's ears, such hard shaking.

The day passed, Pierce saying little beyond what had to be said about eating and washing and doing the chores. It was the longest day Daniel could remember. He was glad when it was over.

The next morning after breakfast, Pierce folded away the quilt Sweet Grass had left behind and gazed for a while at the picture Daniel had drawn of Julia carving and Magpie playing train in the crate. Daniel got up his courage and ventured, "Maybe she'll come back."

"I don't think she can," his father replied. "The gash is deep and it cuts through old scars. Some are of our own making. Others aren't her fault or mine, either," he added.

Daniel waited for him to explain. Instead, his father asked, "You ever see a cockfight?"

Daniel moved his head to say he hadn't.

"You shouldn't. It's ugly," said his father.

Daniel picked at the scab where the splinter had been and offered, "Gram had two roosters got in a fight once over the chickens."

"That's different," said his father. "That's nature taking its course. The fight I saw, men put birds in a ring and gathered around to cheer them on as they spurred and pecked. Each bird was so fixed on killing the other, neither gave any heed to the real enemy right there in plain view. Same here."

Puzzling over the turn in the conversation, Daniel took out his drawing tablet. Just when he thought he didn't know who the enemy was, he caught shades of fear and animosity coiled in pictures he had captured. Drawings of cowboys riding past a stock pen of skinny cattle and men hunched over coffee cups, their boisterous alarm leaping off the page. Pictures that vibrated with thundering hooves and painted horsemen galloping away from Rosebud, rifles aloft. Daniel's eye moved from the mountain of rations piled along a railroad siding in one pencil sketch to the next page where thin-faced old people and women and children fled, leaving their rations behind. The last picture was of Sweet Grass and Magpie on the blanket-padded floor. Daniel had captured a side view of his father as well. His face wasn't visible. But his boots were. They were just inches from Magpie, cowering in her mother's skirts.

You couldn't tell just by looking that it wasn't the boots or the man wearing them that she feared. The enemy wasn't always visible to the naked eye. Daniel leafed through his tablet once more, then watched his father making breakfast at the stove. "Dad? Did Grampa know about the girls?" he asked.

A muscle in Pierce's face jumped. "No. Father was tied to the land," he said, his voice taut. "He never understood why I wasn't. Every letter he wrote, he wanted to know when I was coming home. So I finally did. I patched things up with him and married your mother. Then you came, and it wasn't long before your mother died. A boy misses having a mother. I know I did."

Daniel ducked his head, and rubbed the heat from his eyes.

"I got to thinking Sweet Grass might have figured out the red road wasn't the glory road it once had been," his father continued.

"You met her before you met my mother?"

His father nodded. "I'd asked her once to marry me. She was clinging to the old ways and turned me down. But a little time had passed, and I knew she had a nurturing heart. So I came west and looked her up, thinking I'd send for you if she'd agree to marry me," his father went on, shedding words like glass sheeting rain. "Sure enough, she conceded it was the way of the *Wasicus*. 'Whites,'" he added.

Daniel remembered the word *"Wasicus"* and the way Julia had used it. "Sweet Grass didn't want to be my mother?" he asked in a small voice.

"It wasn't that," said Pierce.

"How come you never sent for me, then?" asked Daniel.

"I wanted to," said his father. "Lots of times. But, in thinking it over, I saw it wasn't fair to you. I couldn't give you what Father and Harmony could. I still can't. Not here, anyway."

It was so quiet, a bird fluttering against the window sounded like a flung stone. "Can we go home, then?" Daniel asked in a whisper.

His father's gaze traveled the quiet room. "I guess it's time," he said finally. "There's nothing keeping me here now."

Chapter Twenty-eight

Daniel's father began that day clearing his things out of the house and disposing of what wouldn't fit in the wagon. They were up before daylight the next morning and headed for the train station in Valentine. It was hard for Daniel to believe he could have his father and home, too. His spirits inched higher with every mile of powdery dust left behind them. "Next stop, Valentine," he said in his best conductor voice.

"Hang on," murmured Pierce.

Rough road threw Daniel against him. He was close enough that he could feel muscles gather as his father braced his feet against the floorboard of the wagon.

They rattled into town with daylight to spare and straight to the station. Daniel stuck close to his father as he bought tickets and unloaded the crate containing his belongings. Daniel's saddlebag was tucked inside it, too, as was Sweet Grass's gift quilt. They left the crate at the station along with a lunch basket for the trip home and his father's grip.

Pierce paid Daniel's breakfast debt at the hotel where they ate supper. He tied up loose ends at the freight company and sold his horse and wagon. They returned to the station just as the train pulled in. The crate had been loaded onto the high-wheeled baggage cart. A baggage man rolled it toward the train. The grip was in the depot where they had left it. But the lunch basket was gone.

"Careless of me to leave it," Pierce said.

"It's a long ride without food," said Daniel.

His father smiled faintly. "I won't let you starve."

Daniel shrugged off his concern and boarded the train at his father's heels. They were on their way home, that's what mattered. He didn't even ask for the window seat. His father settled into it, his hands in his lap, his eyes straight ahead, his bruised and battered boots tapping the floor. Daniel's belly tightened with each *rat-a-tat*.

"Gram's going to be surprised to see you, I'll bet."

His father, face to the window, seemed not to hear. When he looked back at Daniel, his face was tattered patchwork, coming apart at the seams. Then he clamped his jaw tight. His eyes flashed, and he was up and out of his seat.

Alarmed, Daniel bounded up, too. "Dad? Where are you going?"

Pierce pushed Daniel down into the seat and leaned in. The light leaking through the sooty window winked off whiskers that stood apart like sawed-off stumps. "Listen to me, Daniel. Listen! I don't have much time. There is a saying among the Sioux—'The white road leads to the Indian grave.' It's reckless to go. Especially now. I'm getting off this train."

"But you said—"

"I know what I said, and I'm sorry. But you'll be all right. There's Harmony and the whole Tandy clan looking out for *you*."

"No. No!" Daniel struggled, caught in the tangled wool of the same old bad dream. "If you won't come, I'll stay here with you."

"No. Not now," said his father. "Later maybe, when things have settled down. Right now you're going back to your grandmother, where it's safe."

"You don't want me," Daniel blurted, eyes filling.

A muscle jumped on his father's clenched jaw. Wordless, he framed Daniel's head between his hands and turned his face to the train window. A little Indian girl sat on the siding. Her ragged blanket fell open, and her hand shot into a familiar wicker basket.

"Hey! That's ours," began Daniel. Then he stopped and looked closer at her hollow cheeks and bare feet and the gap where she had lost a baby tooth. She was no older than Magpie. He looked and looked and when he looked away and back for his father, he was gone.

The train was a sleepy giant, coming awake. Daniel felt it gathering power through the floorboards of the wooden coach. He looked back at the girl and watched through tears as a skinny dog trotted up and licked her dusty feet. She broke off a piece of biscuit and gave it to the dog.

"Forgot something."

Daniel swiveled in his seat. It was his father, back again, bending toward him from the coach aisle. "Here's your ticket and some folding money to see you home."

Licked, Daniel took it.

"I spoke to the conductor. He'll see to it you get your meals and make sure you get on the right train when you make the first switch. You let the next conductor know you're traveling alone, and he'll look after you, too."

Tears flowed faster than Daniel could wipe them away. His father plucked him out of the seat and into his arms. Daniel buried his face in his neck and hung on tight. There was horse in their embrace. And sweat and dust and tobacco and tears and belongingness.

His father pressed his grizzled check to Daniel's. "I love you, son. Hug Hattie good-bye for me and mind your gram. I'll try to make it home next summer. I promise. You hear that? I promise."

The train rattled and clanged. It chuffed and chooed and lumbered forward. The quilt word turned with the slow-churning wheels. Belongingness. Belongingness.

Daniel wanted to say that he loved him, too. Too full of tears for words, he opened his hands and let him go.

Chapter Twenty-nine

December 30, 1890

"Train's coming. Maybe they'll be on this one," said Jack.

Daniel plucked his lunch pail from the nail on Earl's sap house wall. He and Jack had stopped after school to see if the factory-made buckets Earl had ordered had come yet. There was no sign of Earl or the buckets.

"Earl's charging a dollar a gallon this year," Jack said on the way to the crossing.

A dollar seemed like a lot of money to Daniel. A wagon load of walnuts sold for a dollar. He knew because he had filled seven wagons to earn the money for Gram's bicycle. It was meant as a Christmas surprise. But it hadn't come yet. So he had drawn a picture of a bicycle instead, and framed it for Gram and gave it to her for Christmas. He hadn't told her why. His mouth tipped, thinking how nicely she thanked him.

The apple in Daniel's lunch pail rolled as he loped along at Jack's side.

Jack reached into his trouser pocket for a coin. "I'll toss you for that apple. Heads or tails?" he asked as they crossed the bridge.

"You can have half," said Daniel.

Magpie came to mind as Daniel cut the apple with

Grampa's knife. He had received a letter from his father a week earlier. His father had been to the dance camp several times. He had delivered the pictures Daniel had drawn of the woodlands and Earl's sap house, the tile factory and sawmill and school, and of Miss Jennings and her basket of roots and herbs. He had also passed along Gram's note thanking Sweet Grass for the quilt honoring Grampa Silas. But as yet, Sweet Grass and the girls had not returned home to the cabin.

His father wrote that fear over the Ghost Dance religion was raging. Troops were already on some of the reservations, and were on their way to others. Daniel knew from newspaper accounts that the soldiers had since arrived. That a famous chief had been killed. That Indians had fled for a place in the Badlands called Stronghold while others danced at isolated dance camps on the reservations. Even now, the bluecoats Sweet Grass had so feared were attempting to capture those Gram's newspaper referred to as "hostiles."

In the same paper there was a paragraph about ten cowboys ambushing a party of "hostiles" camped on a creek on the reservation. It didn't say what reservation or what creek. Just that the cowboys had poured a volley of lead from the bluff, killing one "savage" and wounding others. The cowboys, it said, captured seven fine saddles and three good Indian ponies.

Belongingness. It had become a cage around Daniel's heart. The wires bruised and cut with each bit of news from the west. He didn't speak of it to Jack. Jack knew about Sweet Grass and the girls. All the Tandys did now. But there was a difference between knowing *about* and *knowing*.

Daniel wiped his knife blade on his trouser leg as the trees parted for the crossing. The train's steam and smoke ribbon curled toward the sunset as a workman unloaded some empty milk cans, a near-empty mailbag, a crate, and a couple of trunks.

"No buckets. Maybe tomorrow," said Jack.

Daniel mounted the board siding for a closer look at the crate. The wrinkled label bore his name. "Jack!" he shouted. "Look here, it's for me!"

Daniel and Jack carried the mailbag to the store, borrowed a hammer from Mr. Walker, took it back to the crossing, and opened the crate.

"Hey! Wow! Would you look at this? It's red!" Jack exclaimed, running his hands over the bicycle.

Daniel left him trying to ride the bicycle while he returned the hammer.

"Are you headed home?" asked Mr. Walker. "Then take the mail to your grandmother."

There was a newspaper and a postcard. The familiar signature turned Daniel's thoughts to Hattie. In September, he had returned home just in time to see Hattie and her family off for Oklahoma. Anna, after hearing Daniel had been the assistant to three different conductors, couldn't get on the train fast enough. But Hattie sobbed and petted him and said how much she was going to miss him. "I wish I could take you with me," she had cried.

If not for Gram and his promise to look after her, Daniel might have been tempted. But he was glad to be home. Since his return, Gram had been more like her old self. She had quit making gloomy quilts and was knitting now.

Daniel tucked the paper under his arm and read the postcard on his way back to the crossing where Jack was wobbling side to side, fighting to keep from falling as he pedaled the bicycle a safe distance from the tracks.

Dear Aunt Harmony and Daniel,

We have a little farm here, but no house as yet. Matthew is drawing plans for one. He is including a wide front room to be used as a store, as there is no trading center for many miles. The girls and I planted trees last month. Am watering them from the river. We have had rain and high winds and a scare when funnel clouds sailed directly overhead. Our tent blew down, our things were scattered, but we escaped unhurt. We miss everyone.

Love, Hattie and family

"They're living in a tent? No one told me," Jack said when Daniel showed him the postcard. He straddled the bicycle seat with both feet on the ground. "Hold me steady, would you, while I get my balance? I'll show you how I can ride."

The bicycle was a handsome thing. As red as Miss

Jennings's hair with shining fenders and handlebars and nice fat tires. It looked tame enough. But it threw Jack half a dozen times on the way home.

"Your turn," Jack said as the trees gave way to frozen pasture.

Daniel passed him his lunch bucket and the mail and pushed the bicycle home. He called Gram out on the summer porch.

"For me?" she gasped.

"It was supposed to be for Christmas. But it was late getting here," explained Daniel.

"But . . . oh, dear. To think! You've spent all your hard-earned money," stammered Gram. "You shouldn't have. Really. How will I ever learn to ride the thing?"

Injured, Daniel said, "You told Grampa you could. You said bicycles stay put and don't have to be fed and won't bolt at trains," he reminded her.

"Anyway, it rides real easy," chimed Jack. He climbed aboard, pedaled like fury, and collided with a tree.

Daniel heard a sound like a rusty hinge and turned to find Miss Jennings in the open door. It wasn't a squeaking hinge. It was her, laughing. It was a new sound to his ears. His mouth wiggled to hear it.

Jack got up and scratched his head and kicked a tire. "Something's wrong here."

"Nonsense," said Miss Jennings. She turned to Gram. "Go inside and put on a pair of Mr. Tandy's trousers."

"Trousers?" Gram leaned on her cane with one hand and clutched her shawl with the other. "Whatever for?"

"Do you want to learn or don't you?" asked Miss Jennings.

"It's a little chilly," hedged Gram.

"It's quite mild for December," Miss Jennings dismissed her excuse. "The ground isn't even frozen hard."

Gram disappeared inside. When she returned, she was dressed in Grampa's trousers, a short coat, gloves, and a handsome hat firmly tied to her head.

Jack's freckles stood out on his winter-pale cheeks. "This, I got to see."

"An audience is not required," snapped Miss Jennings. "You boys go in the kitchen and don't come out unless I call you."

The Star quilt was draped over Grampa's rocking chair. It had been there since last September when Daniel took it out of the crate and explained to Gram about honor quilts. It took the emptiness from the chair and warmed the room with its bright colors. Daniel flung his coat in that direction and helped himself to the fresh-baked cookies cooling on the table. The pungent aroma of dried herbs tickled his nose as he broke a cookie in half.

"Who made them?" asked Jack.

"Who do you think?" Daniel picked out a few green specks and ate the first half in two bites and the second in one.

Jack sat across the table, looking lean and hungry and bothered. "She may have hexed them."

Daniel left Jack to his silly superstitions, smacked

his lips, and pushed another cookie into his mouth.

Gram's lesson was a short one. She returned to the house, took off her hat and coat and gloves, and sat down to knit.

"How did it go?" Daniel asked Gram.

"She's in one piece, isn't she?" said Miss Jennings.

"Perhaps I'll wait until spring, when there is green grass to catch me," said Gram. "Oops. I dropped a stitch."

Daniel got down on the floor and looked for it. He heard that rusty sound again. Miss Jennings was laughing at him. Gram, too.

"I didn't mean I had dropped it on the floor," said Gram.

"I knew that." Daniel opened Gram's newspaper there on the table and hid his hot face inside.

Or tried to. Miss Jennings snatched the newspaper away. "How am I supposed to put out supper with this spread all over the table?" She folded the front page to the inside and sent him outside with orders to fill the wood box in the parlor.

Daniel didn't give the newspaper another thought until morning when Gram told him there had been trouble on the Pine Ridge Reservation between soldiers and Indians.

"What kind of trouble?" he asked.

"A battle," said Gram. Her taut scars stood out in grim relief. "At a place called Wounded Knee Creek."

Daniel's gaze flew to Grampa's rocking chair and the bright Star quilt.

"Is that close to Dad?"

"I don't know the particulars, Daniel. The papers say that many Indians died trying to get their women and children to safety."

Pine Ridge, Daniel knew, neighbored the Rosebud Reservation.

Chapter Thirty

The newspaper, when it finally fell into Daniel's hands, was grim. Some soldiers had been killed at Wounded Knee. But most of the dead and wounded were Indian. Men, women, children, babies, and old people.

The "skirmish," as the paper called it, was with Big Foot's Miniconjou band. But one article brought the Brulé into it, saying a cavalry captain had to abandon wounded captives when his men were attacked by a large party of Brulé Indians.

Over coming days, the newspaper accounts spoke of scattered Indians and isolated skirmishes and the cavalry's ongoing attempts to restore order. Daniel recalled the Brulé reaction that day at the Rosebud Agency when the *rumor* of troops broke over the camp. Restoring order with troops seemed to him like trying to mend a ripped seam with a knife or a pair of scissors.

Daniel longed for reassurance that his family in the west was safe. Each day he expected word from his father. The days soon added up to a week, and then two, and still there was no message from him.

It was going on three weeks when Daniel dreamed of bloody snow and broken tepees and Captain Fear. He was no ordinary cavalry captain. He rode the clouds, robed in an angry funnel that dropped from the sky. He tore up trees and barns and Gram's house and Tandys, too.

There was drumming in his dream. And dancing buffalo and a pair of snow-white wing-shaped clouds that blotted out Captain Fear. All but his gray cape. It fluttered like a small rumpled curtain over the place where the white wings met and hid something bright. So bright, the cape couldn't altogether conceal it. The light bled over the cape edges, gilding the sky.

Sleep seeped away. The dream faded, but not the drumming. Daniel sat up and listened. It was a fist hitting the front door. He made a light and went downstairs.

It was the storekeeper, Mr. Walker, knocking. "I know it's kind of early," he said as Daniel let him in. "Is your grandmother up?"

"No, sir. Should I get her?"

"I'll leave that to you. A telegram came for her. From your father."

Daniel's pulse jumped as the telegram changed hands. He turned from Mr. Walker and the open door and held the telegram in a pool of yellow lamplight. Two words melted off the pale page:

COMING HOME.

It was signed Pierce, Sweet Grass, Magpie, and Julia.

Epilogue

Lacey had crawled under the quilting frame when Gram told about Pierce changing his mind, and Daniel going home alone. She peeked out as Gram fell silent. "They all came home together?" she said, almost afraid to ask. "Sweet Grass, too?"

"Yes, dear. She and Pierce 'touched the feather,' so to speak, and put their family back together. All of it, this time."

"Daniel, too." Lacey savored the thought. Then she remembered Wounded Knee. "Was Sweet Grass there? And the girls? When they were shooting, I mean?"

"At Wounded Knee? No," said Gram. "Sweet Grass and the girls were fleeing to the Badlands when news reached them about Wounded Knee. Sweet Grass grieved over the senseless tragedy and the plight of her people much the same way Harmony had grieved over Silas. As I understand it, she never truly reconciled herself to life in Illinois. In later years, after the children were grown and Pierce had passed away, she returned to the reservation and lived out the remainder of her life there."

"Did the girls go, too?"

"No. They had families of their own by then."

"That's sad," said Lacey.

"Oh, no! Not at all," said Gram. "Familes are the stitches that hold us all together." She stirred to her feet and returned the Log Cabin quilt to the trunk.

"Wait a second," Lacey said, folding the Star quilt. "You forgot one."

"Belongingness? I didn't forget. I want you to take it home with you. You can keep it until the baby comes." Gram dropped a kiss on Lacey's forehead. "Spread it over your bed and tell me if it clashes."

It wouldn't clash. How could it? It had every color of the rainbow in it. Even a soft peachy shade. Lacy stroked the folds of the old quilt. If there was room in Belongingness for all those colors, there must be a place in her Tandy quilt for orange.

✳ AMERICAN QUILTS SERIES ✳

Activity Pages by Stasia Kehoe

BOOK 3: DANIEL's STORY

Make a Memory: Honor Symbols

Julia carves a wooden horse to honor the memory of Daniel's grandfather, Silas. To try your hand at carving an honor symbol, you will need:

> *A large piece of modeling clay or a large bar*
> *of plain, white soap (Ivory works well)*
> *Carving tools, such as plastic utensils,*
> *wooden skewers, or toothpicks*
> *Texturing tools, such as an old toothbrush,*
> *a nail file, or a lemon zester*
> *Old newspaper*
> *A small paper plate*

[Note: Be sure to get an adult's permission to use the carving and texturing tools you have selected. Adult supervision or assistance may be necessary if using sharp tools.]

Choose a person you would like to honor. Select the animal you would like to carve to honor him or her. Once you have decided what you will carve, look for pictures, other carvings, or even stuffed versions of this animal to help give you ideas for your work. Cover your work surface with the newspaper. Place your clay or soap in the center of the newspaper. Begin by carving the rough shape of the animal, then add texture and detail. [Note: Modeling clay can be dampened and repaired if you make a carving mistake, however, it requires hours or days to harden when carving is completed. Soap carvings are pretty and immediately hard, but soap is fragile and mistakes are difficult to repair. You may want to have a second bar of soap available in case of a major mistake.] Display your completed carving on the paper plate.

Quilting Corner: Colors with "Belongingness"

In *Daniel's Story*, Lacey Tandy wrestles with the idea that she and her new stepsister Sheri belong in the same family. Similarly, Daniel struggles with the notion that his father has another family—other children—so different from himself. Colors that don't seem to belong together give readers a visual image of the feelings Lacey and Daniel share. Yet sometimes very different colors blend together in surprisingly beautiful ways. Use a ruler to divide a large sheet of white paper into four equal squares. Draw a quilt pattern in each square—the pattern can be the same in all four squares, or different. Ask four friends or family members to name their favorite colors, fill a bag with colored pencils or crayons and draw four at random, or choose four colors you would never wear together in an outfit. See if you can fill in your quilt squares with these colors so they seem to belong together. How does this quilting exercise make you think about the word "belonging"?

School Stories: Geography Games

When the weather is too cold for an outdoor recess, Daniel's teacher leads the class in a geography game. Here are some ways you and your friends and family can have fun with a United States map:

—Disappearing States Game. One player uses a Post-It note to cover the name of a state on the map. Other players take turns guessing the name of the covered— "missing"—state.

—West or East? Players sit facing away from the map. One player goes to the map and names two (or more) states. Other players take turns listing the named states in geographical order from west to east.

—Geography Clues. One player stands beside the map and gives a clue about a state (or city or town). Other players take turns guessing the correct name of the state.

Family Tree Time: Cultural Heritage

Out west, Daniel's father, Pierce, has a Native American wife and two children. This mixture of European and Native American cultures in his home can make things difficult, but also interesting and beautiful. Learn more about your cultural background. Does your family history lead you back to a European, Asian, African, or other country? Learn more about your cultural heritage. Use a world map or globe to locate all the continents and/or countries from which your ancestors hail. Have an adult help you prepare some recipes that reflect your heritage and serve your family a feast from your fascinating past.

Presenting the Past: Pioneer Spirit

"Itchy foot" and "wanderlust" are two expressions that describe the feelings of people wanting to head out to the unclaimed American West. Daniel's father went west. Hattie's husband Matthew longs to head west, too. Imagine that you live in Daniel's time and have become caught up in the pioneer spirit. Write a short speech explaining to your family why you want to head west, where you want to go, and what you hope will happen to you. Although the American West is now settled, do you think the pioneer spirit is still alive in the twenty-first century? Where might twenty-first-century pioneers want to go? What might they want to do there?

American Quilt Questions: Growing and Extended Families

Although his father is alive, Daniel lives with his grandparents. Lacey lives in a newly blended family with two stepsisters and a baby on the way. In *Daniel's Story* both Daniel and Lacey wrestle with concerns about belonging in their complicated families.

List the people who care for, or look out for, Daniel. Do you think it would be difficult to have so many "parents"? Explain.

Despite all the love and care surrounding him, what is Daniel planning to do when the story begins? Discuss his reasons for making this plan.

Why is Daniel afraid of Chaldea (Maralee Jennings)? Should he be afraid? In what way is Maralee an important part of Daniel's family?

Does Daniel resent his father's absence? How do you think he would explain his family situation to you if you were his new friend?

What makes Daniel finally attempt the dangerous journey to his father's home? Do you think he was right to try to reach his father?

Daniel's Story

How would you feel if you discovered that an absent parent actually had another family? What questions would you want to ask that parent? Do you think you could learn to get along with a whole new group of sisters or brothers?

BOOK 4: IDA LOU'S STORY

Pigeons cooed from the sunny shoulders of downtown buildings as Ida Young set out for school. She crossed the street between horse-drawn traffic and chuffing motorcars. A foot-high curbing enclosed the lush green courthouse square. Ida stepped up on it, arms outstretched. Lunch rattled in her tin lard pail as she walked the curbing from one end of the block to the other.

General Useful pulled up to the curb and waved to her from the seat of his wagon.

"Morning, General. Watch this!" Ida pirouetted off the curbing and struck a pose. "Ta-da!"

"Bravo, magirl!" he called, his voice as soft as a breeze moving through winter grass. "Are you off to school? Climb up. We'll give you a lift."

"You're headed the other way."

"Josephine won't mind turning around. She's feeling her oats today," said General.

Ida scrambled aboard his brightly painted dray wagon.

"The elephants are coming," said General.

Ida Lou's Story

"Where?" cried Ida, looking both ways.

General's scarred face wouldn't fold into smile wrinkles the way other faces did. But his merry gray eyes gave him away.

"General! You're joking," chided Ida.

"Who, me? Never, magirl!" said General.

In his younger days, General Useful had worked his way up through the circus ranks from candy butcher to lion tamer. He was a scarred patchwork of narrow escapes, with little voice left and nothing outwardly pretty about him. Yet he was almost as dear to Ida as her own runaway daddy.

A block from the school, a group of kids stood in a scraggly line before an old buggy shed.

"What're they looking at?" asked Ida, craning her neck to see.

"I told you, magirl. The elephants are coming. The Wards, too."

"The *Flying* Wards!" Ida clamored down from the wagon and raced ahead. A circus bill covered the whole side of the buggy shed. She swung around and hollered back, "You *weren't* joking, they really *are* coming!"

General winked and tipped his hat and shook the lines over Josephine's back.

Ida gazed at the snarling lions and capering clowns and tumblers and tamers. She closed her eyes and smelled sawdust and peanuts and animals. Heard cracking whips and silvery trumpets and high-stepping horses circling the ring. *Gallopy-trot.*

The jabbering of schoolmates faded. The street

retreated. The nearby church and homes and passing streetcars, too, until it was just Ida and the circus bill. It seemed to her for a moment as if the scene on the buggy shed wall were real and the city were made of paper.

Then the first bell rang with stale offerings of science and sums and fearful news of the war in Europe. Boys and girls crossed the street, heading toward the yawning schoolhouse doors. Still, Ida couldn't pull herself away. "Dizzying, death-defying heights," she read aloud. "Dauntless, daring, intre-intre—"

"Intrepid."

Ida swung around. A slender boy with slicked-down hair had slipped up behind her. He'd missed a clump of yellow hair with the brush. It stood up like a dandelion, just behind of his center part. "Intrepid," he said again. "It means fearless."

"I know," said Ida, though she hadn't.

The boy read the circus bill out loud without stumbling over a single word.

"Have you got money for a ticket?" he asked.

Ida tipped her chin and didn't answer.

"Me, either," he said. "But we've got a whole month to earn some."

"Together, you mean?" asked Ida, surprised. At her school, boys didn't have much to do with girls except to dip their braids in inkwells or let them be nurses in their trench warfare games.

"Two heads are better than one," said the yellow-haired boy.

"Hands, too," said Ida. "What's your name?"

Ida Lou's Story

"Sylvester Baumgart. My friends call me Slick."

"Did your family just move here?"

"My brother got drafted, so I moved in with my Aunt Pliney. My folks are gone," he added.

Gone could mean dead. Or it could mean just that, up and gone. Ida didn't like being asked family questions. So she didn't ask him.

"Who are you?" said Slick.

"Florida Louisa Young. Ida Lou, for short."

"What grade are you in?"

"Fifth. How about you?"

"Sixth." Slick put his hand over his sandy eyebrows and stepped closer. His little finger grazed the top of her head. "You know what? You *are* short."

"So is she." Ida pointed out the dark-haired beauty on the buggy shed wall.

"Jennie Ward? You like her?"

"She's the best."

"What do you know! The Wards are my favorites, too," said Slick. "The men do harder tricks. But girls look prettier coming off a trapeze."

Before Ida could protest, Slick spun around and did handsprings down the walk. He was as quick and light as if he had leaped off the circus bill.

"Do you take tumbling at the Y?" asked Ida, catching up with him.

"Where's that?"

"The YMCA. It's just down the street from our building," said Ida. "I see boys coming and going all the time. Circus people, too. That's where they practice after the season is over and they come home for the winter."

"Do you ever see Eddie Ward?" asked Slick.

"No. Not since he built his own flying barn east of town."

"I'll have to check that out," said Slick. He pecked on her lard pail lunch bucket. "What have you got in here?"

"Hard-boiled eggs. How about you?"

"Biscuits. We could put them together and have an egg sandwich."

"First bell has already rung," said Ida.

"Don't worry. If you're late, just tell your teacher I'm new and you're helping me find my way to class," said Slick. He climbed up on the mounting block in front of the church next to the school and opened his lunch pail.

Ida didn't like the word 'tardy.' Especially when it was on a note home to Mom. But she didn't want Slick thinking she lacked gumption.

"Are you going to peel the egg or shall I?" asked Slick.

Maybe if she ate fast . . . "I will," said Ida. She scrambled up beside him.

"I figure it'll cost us thirty-five, maybe fifty cents apiece to get into the circus," he said. "Any ideas how we can earn it?"

"I sweep up hair for the barber in our building sometimes. He pays me a nickel," said Ida.

Slick split his biscuit with a pocketknife while she peeled an egg. "You live downtown?" At Ida's nod, he asked, "Do you know all the merchants?"

"Businesspeople, you mean? In our building, I do," said Ida, giving him the hard-boiled egg to slice. He ate a bite and put the rest on the sandwich.

"Would any of them hire us?"

"We could ask," said Ida.

"It's settled, then."

"When?" asked Ida.

"How about Saturday? That'll give us a whole day," reasoned Slick.

The last bell rang. Ida crammed her share of sandwich in her mouth and leaped to the ground, spewing crumbs.

But to her surprise, Slick was right about her excuse for being late. It worked.

Printed in the United States
109648LV00001B/34-36/A